PRAISE FOR

RED LETTER CHRISTIANS

Tony writes this book with the Bible in one hand and the newspaper in the other, reminding us that our faith must affect how we live in this world. Tony helps us read America biblically, with the eyes of Jesus, rather than reading the Bible through the eyes of America. And be assured that this book is not just about how to vote in November . . . this is about how we vote every single day.

SHANE CLAIBORNE
Urban Monastic, Activist, Red Letter Christian and Author of *Jesus for President*

This book not only knocks your socks off, it puts your feet in sandals and helps you follow Jesus. *Red Letter Christians* is full of fascinating facts and insights, and we are all once again reminded that practical acts of loving our neighbor transform us into personal expressions of the Christ we worship.

JOEL HUNTER
Senior Pastor of Northland, A Church Distributed, Longwood, Florida
Author of *A New Kind of Conservative*

Evangelical Christianity has always been an essentially activist faith, and it loses its way when it forgets this activist edge. In *Red Letter Christians*, Tony Campolo challenges all of us to recover the active nature of our faith and to let it infiltrate all aspects of our lives. He continues to have a prophetic voice.

TONY JONES
Author of *The New Christians: Dispatches from the Emergent Frontier*
National Coordinator of Emergent Village (www.emergentvillage.com)

I have been inspired by Tony's work for decades. But somehow I think his voice is needed now more than ever. With "Campolian" passion and insight, *Red Letter Christians* prods, challenges, questions, invites and instructs us to be people who love and live the words of Jesus.

BRIAN MCLAREN
Author (brianmclaren.net)

Tony Campolo has been a powerful voice for biblical justice for decades. One need not agree with every word to recognize *Red Letter Christians* as another important call to action.

RONALD J. SIDER
President of Evangelicals for Social Action
Author of *Rich Christians in an Age of Hunger*

TONY CAMPOLO

A CITIZEN'S GUIDE TO FAITH & POLITICS

RED LETTER CHRISTIANS

Regal

From Gospel Light
Ventura, California, U.S.A.

Published by Regal
From Gospel Light
Ventura, California, U.S.A.
www.regalbooks.com
Printed in the U.S.A.

Library of Congress Cataloging-in-Publication Data
Campolo, Anthony.
Red letter Christians / Tony Campolo.
p. cm.
ISBN 978-0-8307-6865-3 (trade paper)
1. Evangelicalism–United States. 2. Christianity and culture–United States.
3. United States–Church history. I. Title.
BR1642.U5C34 2008
277.3'083–dc22
2007034012

Dedicated to Loretta Kier,
whose love for us and our love for her
made her part of our family.

CONTENTS

SECTION FOUR

The Economic Issues

SECTION FIVE

The Government Issues

Concluding Perspectives

FOREWORD

When we went to Nashville on the *God's Politics* book tour, we didn't do a lecture—we did a concert! Ashley Cleveland, Buddy Miller, Emmy Lou Harris and Jars of Clay all played and sang, and I preached. We sold out the historic Belcourt Theatre twice in one night and had a lot of fun.

While there, I did some interviews, but one was particularly memorable. "I'm a secular Jewish country-music songwriter and disk jockey," my interviewer on a Nashville radio station said. "But I love your stuff and have been following your book tour." Then he told me he believed we were starting a new movement, but he noticed we hadn't come up with a name for it yet. "I've got an idea for you," he said. "I think you should call yourselves 'The Red Letter Christians.' You know those Bibles that highlight the words of Jesus in red letters? I love the red-letter stuff. The rest I could do without."

When I told Tony Campolo that story, he almost jumped out of his seat. And when Tony gets excited—watch out! He got excited because Tony *is* a Red Letter Christian, and has been for a very long time. You might even call him the "godfather" of the Red Letter Christians . . . after all, he is Italian.

We Christians have a serious problem. Most people have the idea that Christians and the Church are supposed to stand for the same things that Jesus did. When we don't stand for the things Jesus did, people get confused and disillusioned. Like I say, it's a problem.

Jesus Himself is a problem. He's a problem for the Wall Street traders, the Madison Avenue advertisers, the media moguls of Times Square, the Hollywood stars whose limos cruise Sunset Strip, the K Street lobbyists and the powerful people on Pennsylvania Avenue who strive to maintain American imperial power. Closer to home, Jesus is a problem for many churches on Main Street who have substituted the values of the culture for His teachings.

In spite of what the Church has done and left undone, millions of people, religious or not, discover that Jesus remains the most compelling figure in the world today. The Church may not be much more credible than the stock brokers, the advertisers, the media, the special interests or the politicians, but Jesus still stands far above the rest of the crowd. Somehow, Jesus has survived all of us who profess His name but too often forget most of what He said.

For example, when Jesus tells us that He will regard the way we treat the hungry, the homeless, the immigrant, the poor family, the sick and the prisoner as if we were treating Him that way, it likely means that He would not think ignoring them is good domestic policy. Or when He tells us to "love your enemies" and that "blessed are the peacemakers," it might be hard to persuade Him to join "wars against terrorism" with so much "collateral damage" to civilians. And in the wake of U.S. military scandals from Guantanamo Bay to Abu Ghraib, Jesus would probably have something to say to those who torture America's enemies.

It is almost as if the real message of Jesus has been kept a secret, utterly disguised by prosperity pastors, television evangelists and radio talk show hosts who preach a conservative American religion across the world, giving a very different impression of Christianity than Jesus taught. The good news is that the "secret" is getting out. Jesus is breaking through, drawing an alienated generation raised in the churches back to His teachings and attracting many outside the religious community to a message they never heard from the pews.

Perhaps because our culture and politics have gone so off course, with values so contrary to those of Jesus, more and more people intuitively recognize that His vision of God's kingdom—a new world of compassion, justice, integrity and peace—is the Good News they've been searching and waiting for.

A fellowship of Christian authors, speakers and activists has recently come together as the Red Letter Christians. We affirm the authority of the whole Bible, not just the explicit sayings of Jesus, often found highlighted in red. We haven't formed a new organization. We are not from any one church or tradition. We have no particular political agenda.

But we believe that the "red letters" of Jesus need to be focused on again. We feel a calling together in this historical moment to bring back the distinctive message of Jesus for our time, for our world and for the critical issues we face today.

As a fellow Red Letter Christian, Tony Campolo knows that people of faith should not be in the pocket of any political party—that God is not a Republican or a Democrat. So why do we often find this basic wisdom ignored whenever we discuss faith and politics in our churches? It's time for us to move beyond this silliness.

Rather than being loyal partisans, Christians engaging politics should be the ultimate swing vote, holding both sides accountable to a broader moral vision. The apostle Paul told early believers living in the heart of the Roman Empire to conform to a different moral logic than that which the world had to offer. The same is no less true for us today.

Why? Because believers are informed by a different moral compass, a compass whose true north points us toward Bethlehem rather than Rome (or in the case of many American Christians, Bethlehem rather than Washington, DC).

Over the years Tony Campolo has been my dear friend, colleague and co-conspirator for faith and justice. He's devoted his life to reshaping how those of us in the Church engage the most heartbreaking realities facing the world today.

With the maturity and depth only an elder statesman can provide, Tony brings his acute moral clarity to issues ranging from abortion to environmental stewardship, global poverty to gay marriage . . . and everything in between. He reminds us that as Christians living in a democracy where we have the ability to participate, we also have a responsibility to engage. In the red-letter words of Jesus, "To whom much is given . . . much will be required" (Luke 12:48, *NKJV*).

The question is not, Should Christians be involved in politics? The real question is, How? To this end, Tony offers a radically simple solution. It happens to be the same solution Jesus of Nazareth offered His first disciples: "Follow Me."

Fixed on this compass, Red Letter Christians are those who dare to take Jesus seriously; those who believe that if He said it, He meant it; and if He meant it, then we must live it.

This book reminds us that our primary allegiance as Christians is not to a country or a flag, an empire or a king, a president or a political party. Instead, we belong to the One who first spoke the letters in red.

These words—the red letters—must humbly guide our public witness and political decision-making as people of faith.

Jim Wallis
Founder and editor of *Sojourners Magazine*
Author of *God's Politics: Why the Right Gets It Wrong and the Left Doesn't Get It*

PREFACE

Nothing is so dependable in politics as change, which is what made writing this book so difficult. By the time you read it, many of the issues I discuss herein might be passé or resolved, and new political issues may have moved to center stage. Nevertheless, I did my best to focus on the topics and stories you are reading about in today's newspapers and viewing on 24-hour cable or Internet news.

There is a growing consensus among the political science professors I talk with on college and university campuses that the United States of America is passing through some kind of watershed period, and that when this decade is over, the rest of the world will no longer view us as they once did. How we use our power will make America either the most despised or the most admired nation on the planet.

Your vote has much to do with which of those two alternatives becomes a reality.

In the past you have been told that voting is important, that it is your patriotic responsibility to get out on Election Day and cast your ballot. You even know that carrying out this civic responsibility is a Christian obligation. But I contend that, given our particular place in history, such statements are not just slogans or political mantras. Given what we Americans are facing in the days ahead, both domestically and internationally, these statements carry a weight greater than ever before.

In this book I've tried to be "fair and balanced," as they say on Fox News. As to how well I have carried out that responsibility, I leave you to judge. I have tried to go beyond unsubstantiated opinions and give you validated facts to back up what I say. This book has more sources cited than any other book I have written. Having said that, I'm not certain that all of them are reliable. Some of them are secondary. Some come from newspaper articles and electronic media. What I hope they show, however, is that I have not pulled my assertions out of thin air. You may not agree that all my sources can be trusted, but at least you have a good survey of where I get the information that is grounds for my views.

When it comes to research, I have to give all kinds of credit to Robert Gauthier, who works with me in the ministries of Evangelical Association for the Promotion of Education (EAPE). Robert did a great deal of the research that went into producing this book, but he did not work alone—several student assistants helped him: Benjamin Lander, Amy Smith, Kurt Focht, Evan Hewitt, Ben Cressy and Bronte Hughes.

Overcoming my shortcomings with the English language were proofreaders who included my wife (who suffered long and hard making corrections) and Mary Darling, a professor at Spring Arbor University. The key person to any success this book may enjoy is Aly Hawkins, the excellent editor assigned to me by Regal Books. Without any exaggeration, Aly proved to be among the best editors I have ever had.

What makes me a rarity these days is that I do not use a computer. Everything I write is long hand. Handwritten pages for this book were sent to my secretary-typist, Sarah Blaisdell. You would not be reading this if not for her hard work, and I will always be grateful to her.

Coordinating this whole complex operation has been my personal assistant, James Warren. My wife will tell you that without James, not only this book but also my whole professional life would be in chaos. To James and all of the above, I say, "Thanks!"

I hope you find this book helpful. Beyond that, I hope it challenges you to be engaged in the political process. And above all else, I hope that as you read and reflect on the biblical imperatives that prescribe my political positions, you are prompted to study the Scriptures for yourself. Perhaps you will not agree with my reading of the Bible. But let us agree that this ancient Book speaks with timeliness and truth to the concerns we now face as a nation.

Tony Campolo

AN INTRODUCTION

The term "Evangelical" has been given meanings it does not deserve. In most secular settings, if you define yourself as an Evangelical, certain assumptions will be made about you that may not be true. There may even be assumptions you resent.

Recently on the campus of an Ivy League university, I asked some students what they thought Evangelicals believed. None of them gave any indication that they defined Evangelicals by their theological convictions. Instead, the general consensus among these students was that Evangelicals are those Christians who are anti-gay, anti-feminist, anti-environmentalists, anti-gun-control, pro-war, right-wing ideologues. There is little doubt that the secular media is largely responsible for this view of Evangelicals, in that it has chosen those who espouse such convictions to be the Evangelical spokespersons. The press seldom turns to political moderates when they want comments on religiously charged social issues.

To set the record straight, there was a time when the leaders of the Evangelical movement were the *avant garde* of progressive politics—anything *but* right-wing conservatives. The likes of Charles Finney, who could be called the Billy Graham of the nineteenth century, and William Jennings Bryan, the darling of Evangelicals in the early twentieth century, were rousing voices of political progressivism.

Charles Finney's powerful preaching won to his side a group of firebrand followers who became a major force in the American antislavery movement. When his salvation-seeking listeners came down the aisles when Finney gave the invitation to accept Christ, he asked them immediately if they were willing to become abolitionists. So far as Finney was concerned, given the times in which he lived, not to work to end slavery was not to be a serious Christian. In addition, his disciples provided much of the leadership for the then-emerging feminist movement. Contemporary feminists who often view Evangelicals as enemies to their cause might be surprised to learn that their movement has roots in Evangelicalism, and that the earliest feminist gatherings were held in churches.

William Jennings Bryan is labeled as a kind of foolhardy reactionary because of his role in the famous 1922 Scopes Trial. As you may recall, he was the prosecutor of John Thomas Scopes, who dared to break a Tennessee law that forbade the teaching of Charles Darwin's theory of evolution in public schools. Recently, a negative image of Bryan has been promulgated because of the film *Inherit the Wind*. Clarence Darrow, one of the foremost lawyers of the day, was Scopes's defense attorney, and in the movie he makes Bryan look like a buffoon when Bryan himself takes the stand to defend his belief in a six-day creation. In reality, to the chagrin of many creationists, he had no problem with a belief that God may have taken eons of time to create the universe. Bryan's concerns about evolution went far deeper than that of an ignorant, anti-science religious nut, as he was portrayed in the film. He understood the social implications of Darwin's theory better than Darrow did. He recognized that what Darwin proposed on the biological level, when applied on the societal level, might legitimize an ideology that supports the survival of the fittest, with all of its dire implications. Bryan was able to envision the kind of society that Social Darwinism would create—the kind of exploitation that comes from unbridled capitalism, for instance—and chose to war against it. His conviction that common people are of ultimate value was what lay behind his opposition to the Robber Barons, whose only ethic was determined by what their political and economic power would allow. He was committed to protecting common citizens from such unscrupulous corporate giants, and promoted the needed anti-trust legislation that reined in destructive monopolies of the business world. It was Bryan's call for government controls on industry that generated enough public support to bring an end to factories and mines utilizing child labor to maximize profits.

And if his industrial activism wasn't enough, Bryan's support for the suffrage movement was essential in gaining the right for women to vote, and he was the only member of a president's cabinet ever to resign because of his convictions about war. As a pacifist, he was convinced that he could not serve as Secretary of State when the United States entered World War I. His position certainly stands in contrast to the Religious Right pro-militarists who seem to dominate the contemporary Evangelical scene.

Challenging the popular image of Evangelicals is one of the purposes of this book. I want it to be known that there are millions of us who espouse an evangelical theology, but who reject being classified as part of the Religious Right. We don't want to make Jesus into a Republican.

On the other hand, we want to say loud and clear that we don't want to make Jesus into a Democrat, either.

Early twentieth-century playwright and social critic George Bernard Shaw once said that God created us in His image—and we decided to return the favor! Clearly there are those on the Religious Right who would make Jesus into a Republican and an incarnation of their political values. And on the other side of the aisle, there are those who would make Jesus into a Democrat who espouses their particular liberal agenda. But Jesus refuses to fit into any of our political ideologies. Transcending partisan politics, Jesus calls us to make judgments about social issues as best we can when we vote, and to do so in accord with our best understanding of God's will. In doing so, we are to avoid partisan politics that lead to unnecessary, unproductive and even dangerous divisions.

At election time when you are asked, "Are you a Democrat or a Republican?" your answer should be, "Name the issue!" On any specific social or political issue, you must be ready and willing to work out which party and/or candidate best represents your convictions.

This, of course, will make voting into a difficult decision-making process. But who said following Jesus was easy?

This book is in no way intended to tell the reader *how* to vote, but instead to raise issues that will be highlighted in coming elections and to explore the implications of faith for us and our stance on these issues. Needless to say, my own preferences will be easily discerned, but I hope that beyond my own opinions you will find useful information and biblical perspectives that will help you in discerning for yourself how you should vote.

LIVING BY THE RED LETTERS

SECTION ONE

CHAPTER 1

WHO ARE RED LETTER CHRISTIANS?

Given the general contemporary meanings and connotations ascribed to the word "Evangelical," a group of us who are speakers and authors and who share an evangelical theology got together and confessed that we have a hard time applying the label to ourselves anymore. This group included Brian McLaren, a leader in the emerging church movement; Richard Rohr, the well-known Catholic writer and speaker; Cheryl Sanders, a prominent African-American pastor; Noel Castellanos, a strong voice in the Latino community; and Jim Wallis and Duane Shank, two key leaders of the Sojourners Community and the Call to Renewal movement. We struggled to come up with a new name to define ourselves.

As you can well imagine, we had a hard time. We did not want to call ourselves "progressive Evangelicals," because that might imply a value judgment on those who do not share our views. We batted around several possible names, and then, in the midst of our discussions, the name "Red Letter Christians" was proposed.

Actually, the name was first used by a secular Jewish country-western disc jockey in Nashville, Tennessee. During a radio interview with Jim Wallis, the DJ tried to nail down Jim's particular breed of Christianity and finally said, "So you're one of those Red Letter Christians—you know—who's really into those verses in the New Testament that are in red letters."

Jim answered, "That's right!" And with that, he spoke for all of us.

By calling ourselves Red Letter Christians, we are alluding to those old versions of the Bible wherein the words of Jesus are printed in red.

In adopting the name, we are saying that we are committed to living out the things that Jesus taught.

The message in those red letters is radical, to say the least. If you don't believe me, just read Jesus' words in the Sermon on the Mount, found in Matthew 5–7. In the red letters of this sermon, Jesus calls us to an "upside-down Kingdom," far away from the dominant values of the modern American consciousness. For instance, Jesus tells us that we cannot be sucked into a system that seeks life's meaning and satisfaction in materialism and self-gratification while still claiming to serve God. Furthermore, He challenges many of the social policies that too many Evangelicals fail to question. Consider the fact that He calls us to be merciful (see Matt. 5:7), which has strong implications for how we should think about capital punishment—and since Jesus also tells us to love our enemies, we probably shouldn't consider it an option (see Matt. 5:44). These words should cause us to examine our attitudes about war, as well. Most important, when we reflect on all Jesus had to say about caring for the poor and oppressed, committing ourselves to His red-letter message just might drive us to see what we can do politically to help those He called "the least of these" (see Matt. 25:31-46).

It seemed to us newly named Red Letter Christians at one of our early meetings that Evangelicals often evade what Jesus said in those red letters in the Bible, and that this evasion lends some credence to Mahatma Gandhi's claim that everybody in the world knows what Jesus taught—except for Christians!

We decided to refute that claim. And we began with the grounding essentials that make us *Christian*.

First, Red Letter Christians hold to the same theological convictions that define Evangelicals. We believe in the doctrines set down in the Apostles' Creed, which states the central beliefs the Church has held over centuries:

I believe in God the Father Almighty, Maker of heaven and earth.
And in Jesus Christ His only Son our Lord;
who was conceived by the Holy Ghost, born of the Virgin Mary,
suffered under Pontius Pilate, was crucified, dead and buried;
He descended into hell; the third day He rose again from the dead;
He ascended into heaven, and sits on the right hand
of God the Father Almighty; from thence He shall come
to judge the quick and the dead.
I believe in the Holy Ghost; the holy catholic Church;
the communion of saints; the forgiveness of sins;
the resurrection of the body; and the life everlasting.

Second, we are Christians with a very high view of Scripture. The writers of Scripture, we believe, were invaded by the Holy Spirit and were uniquely guided by God as they wrote, providing us with an infallible guide for faith and practice. We emphasize the "red letters" because we believe that you can only understand the rest of the Bible when you read it from the perspective provided by Christ.

Third—and this is most important—we claim that the historical Jesus can be alive and present to each and every person, and that salvation depends on yielding to Him and inviting Him to be a vital, transforming presence in our lives. The same Son of God described in the Apostles' Creed will spiritually invade any of us who will receive Him (see John 1:12) to initiate in us an ongoing process whereby we are transformed into persons who are increasingly like Him (see 1 John 3:2).

From those essentials, we turned to what priorities make us *Red Letter*. What differentiates Red Letter Christians from other Christians is our passionate commitment to social justice—hence, our intense involvement in politics. This involvement sometimes makes us controversial.

Whereas some leading Evangelical spokespersons focus almost all their attention on preventing gay marriages and overturning past

Supreme Court rulings on abortion, Red Letter Christians, while recognizing the great importance of these issues, embrace a broad range of social concerns, giving special attention to legislation that provides help for the poor and hope for the oppressed. Declaring that there are more than 2,000 verses of Scripture that call us to express love and justice for those who are poor and oppressed, we promote legislation that turns biblical imperatives into social policy. We again concur with Gandhi when he said, "Those who say religion has nothing to do with politics do not know what religion is."

An example of this elemental relationship between faith and politics was William Wilberforce, a political leader who became a leading influence in the British Parliament for the abolition of slavery. The recent motion picture *Amazing Grace* gives us a portrait of this relentless man of faith, whose religious convictions compelled his sustained campaign against slavery. The idea that Wilberforce's religion should have no place in the civic sphere would never have occurred to him—it was his faith that thrust him into politics!

Poverty is a major concern for Red Letter Christians. We find it significant that in Christ's story of the rich man and Lazarus, as recorded in Luke 16:19-31, the sin that warrants the rich man's condemnation is that he "feasted sumptuously" while remaining indifferent to the poor man at his gate. Given such biblical illustrations of God's concerns, we contend that we have a God-given responsibility to share with the poor and to be a voice for the voiceless oppressed. On the day of judgment, the Lord will not ask theological questions so much as He will ask if we fulfilled our social obligations. He will ask whether or not we fed the hungry, clothed the naked, received and cared for aliens, and brought deliverance to captive peoples (see Matt. 5:31-46).

Several years ago I was having dinner in a restaurant in Port-au-Prince, Haiti. I was seated comfortably at a table next to the front window of the restaurant, ready to begin enjoying my meal, when I realized I was being watched. With their noses pressed flat against the glass, three raggedy, dirty Haitian boys stared at the food on my plate. Their hair was rust-colored because of a lack of protein and they had the distended stomachs that give evidence of extreme malnutrition. Their eyes, riveted on my food, were disturbing. To say the least.

The waiter, recognizing how upset I was, moved quickly to pull down the window shade. "Don't let them bother you! Enjoy your meal!" he said.

As if I could.

In a sense, isn't that what we all do? Don't those of us who live comfortable lives "pull down the shade"? Don't we hide ourselves from those millions of desperate people who press their noses against the glass barrier that separates them from sustenance we have on this side? Don't we, for the most part, ignore the 6 million children who die each year of either starvation or diseases related to malnutrition?[1]

We Red Letter Christians are committed to raising the window shades and confronting the needs of the poor. We are Christians who will press for social policies that address and meet these needs.

Presently the United States allocates less than four-tenths of 1 percent (0.4%) of its federal budget to address world poverty.[2] While much has been done by voluntary organizations, and especially by churches and other faith-based organizations, the richest people on the face of the earth ought to have a government that does better than that. Americans make up 4.5 percent of the world's population and consume more than 40 percent of the world's resources.[3] Given that reality, there is something terribly amiss when our national budget ranks second to last of the 22 industrialized nations for assistance to the world's poor.[4]

Poverty, however, is not just a malady that affects developing nations. Extreme poverty is an increasing reality here in our own country. You don't have to go to the Third World anymore to visit the Third World. Third-World conditions exist in urban neighborhoods in cities across America and in the lonely hills of Appalachia.

If you need a case study to illustrate the dire consequences of poverty for its victims, take a look at Camden, New Jersey. In that city, just across the Delaware River from Philadelphia (the birthplace of American independence), the ravages of poverty are in blatant evidence.

One out of every seven houses has been abandoned over the last decade. Conditions in the city are so bad that those who could, got out of town—even though buyers for their property could not be found.[5]

Only 13.6 percent of families with children under 18 are headed by married couples.[6]

In a city of 80,000, there are only two emergency rooms.[7]

Crime is rampant—year after year, Camden registers the highest per-capita murder rate of any city in the nation.[8]

More than 10,000 outsiders drive into the city each day to buy drugs.[9]

If you are a 15-year-old male, there is a nearly 40-percent probability that you will spend two years in jail before you are 30.[10]

Recently, both the mayor and the district attorney were arrested on charges of ties to the Mafia.[11]

The school system is in shambles—there was so much inefficiency and corruption in the administration that the state's board of education had to intervene and take over.[12]

Less than 50 percent of those who attend the two major high schools in Camden ever graduate,[13] and there is no telling how many of them are functionally illiterate.

Various industries that once provided jobs are gone. Campbell's Soup, RCA, Whitman's Candies and Sheaffer Pens have all moved out. The downtown stores are closed and banks have relocated. The unemployment rate in Camden now stands at approximately 15 percent.[14]

Those who say that the problems of places like Camden can be resolved in a libertarian fashion—with churches and other voluntary organizations meeting the needs of the city without government programs and dollars—have a hard time convincing people like me.

I strongly believe that while churches and charities have done incredible work to alleviate the suffering of the needy, they cannot provide universal healthcare or guarantee a minimum wage. These fall under the province of government.

At election time, questions should be asked about what candidates propose for places such as Camden. We dare not walk away from such social chaos.

Edmund Burke, the British social philosopher, once said, "All that is necessary for evil to triumph is for good men to do nothing." Most of us have heard those words at one time or another. But now is the time for us to respond to Burke's ultimatum.

Red Letter Christians accept that challenge as a call to political action. We are people who, when the death knell sounds on behalf of the poor and socially downtrodden peoples of the world, do not ask for whom the bell tolls. The prophetic words of the poet John Donne resound in our ears: "The bell tolls for thee!"

Consider the fact that 47 million Americans have no medical coverage, and the insurance situation for the poorest Americans is worsening every day.[15]

The gap between the rich and the poor widens each day. Corporate executives now have incomes that are 400-times greater than the average worker.[16]

Given inflation, the buying power of the typical worker has dropped dramatically over the past 15 years.[17]

Every day, thousands more of our fellow citizens fall below the poverty level.[18]

Foreclosures on house mortgages are rising exponentially while homelessness has become a national epidemic. Presently it is estimated that more than 3.5 million people—1.5 million children among them—experience homelessness every year.[19] Those who provide shelters for people living on the streets claim that they cannot meet the demand.

At least 20 percent of homeless people are military veterans, shameful evidence of our hypocrisy when we talk patriotically about honoring those who have served in the armed services.[20] What's even more shocking is that half of all homeless people are women and children.[21]

There are Evangelicals who argue against environmentalism, claiming that global warming is a myth (or at least grossly exaggerated), and that environmental concerns distract Christians from those matters that should fully occupy our moral and political attention: gay marriage and abortion. They seem to have ignored the biblical assertion that God didn't create land and sea to be abused and misused for our own selfish purposes. These brothers and sisters in Christ do not give adequate attention to God's call to be stewards of the natural world, not just for our own sakes, but also for the good of others. Yes, the environment is a justice issue. It's easy to disregard the mounting urgency of environmental issues when one doesn't have to live in places where noxious fumes from oil refineries and toxic waste make for increased cases of cancer and lung disease, or where rapidly changing climate threatens the community's livelihood.

These Christians don't understand that environmental degradation in the developing world is a major contributor to extreme poverty. In Haiti, for example, there has been incredible deforestation over a very short period of time, directly contributing to the hunger of Haiti's citizens. There are 84 percent fewer trees standing today than 20 years ago.[22] Consequently, when there are heavy rains in Haiti, there is vast soil erosion, which dramatically diminishes the capacity of the land to grow good crops. Not to mention that when hurricane season comes, torrential downpours create flooding and landslides that wipe out entire villages.

Another example of the developing world hit hardest by environmental carelessness is in Africa, where changing weather patterns contribute to desertification. The Sahara is expanding across the African continent at the rate of three miles a year, exacerbating widespread droughts and famine, and exponentially reducing tillable land.[23]

It is the epitome of selfishness for those Christians who are least affected by the destructive exploitation of the earth to suggest that environmental issues ought not to be among our primary political concerns.

We Red Letter Christians consider ignoring the necessity of legislation to address such careless disregard as more than a disgrace: We call it sinful. And if some of those old Hebrew prophets were around today, they would have a lot to say about it.

CHAPTER 2

A BIBLICAL APPROACH TO POLITICS

Jesus would have gone over well in our modern media age, when complicated political messages are reduced to sound bites. If a reporter had asked Jesus to spell out His platform in a brief and easy-to-understand sentence, Jesus would have said, "I have come to declare that the Kingdom of God is at hand!"

In each of the synoptic Gospels, we read that this is the proclamation Jesus made to initiate His ministry (see Matt. 4:17; Mark 1:15; Luke 4:43). Nearly all of His parables were about this Kingdom. When He taught His disciples to pray, He taught them to ask the Father for this new social order to come "on earth as it is in heaven" (Matt. 6:10). And at the end of His ministry, just prior to His ascension to the Father, He wanted to be sure His followers would not lose sight of the mission's essence, so He *again* taught them things concerning the Kingdom.

First-century Jews, to whom Jesus initially addressed His message of the Kingdom, had a firm grasp on what He was talking about. For centuries, they'd had prophets who defined for them in very concrete ways what the Kingdom would be like. As a case in point, Isaiah prophesied:

> No more shall there be in it
> an infant that lives but a few days,
> or an old person who does not live out a lifetime;
> for one who dies at a hundred years will be considered a youth,

and one who falls short of a hundred will be considered accursed.
They shall build houses and inhabit them;
they shall plant vineyards and eat their fruit.
They shall not build and another inhabit;
they shall not plant and another eat;
for like the days of a tree shall the days of my people be,
and my chosen shall long enjoy the work of their hands.
They shall not labor in vain,
or bear children for calamity;
for they shall be offspring blessed by the Lord
and their descendants as well.
Before they call I will answer,
while they are yet speaking I will hear.
The wolf and the lamb shall feed together,
the lion shall eat straw like the ox;
but the serpent its food shall be dust!
They shall not hurt or destroy on all my holy mountain,
says the LORD (Isa. 65:20-25).

The Jews knew that it was not about some "pie in the sky by and by" escape from the bad old world. Instead, the Kingdom was to be a new kind of society, wherein the effects of poverty and physical suffering would be no more.

A day will come when starvation and diseases will no longer take the lives of infants (v. 20).

On that day, mothers will not worry that they have lovingly raised their children into their teenage years only to have them blown away by vicious street gangs or dissipated by drugs (v. 23).

When the Kingdom of our Lord comes in its fullness, old people will live out long lives without having to choose between buying food and purchasing overpriced prescription drugs (v. 20).

The millions of people who are made into homeless refugees because of wars, and those right here in the U.S. who find themselves without roofs over their heads, will cheer in God's coming Kingdom, because houses will be built for everyone (vv. 21-22).

Those desperate would-be immigrants who sneak across our borders hoping to find work will hear the deliriously joyful announcement that God has planned a new socio-economic order, wherein everyone who wants to work will have a job (v. 21).

And for environmentalists concerned about what we are doing to planet Earth, here is the assurance that a time will come when people will not "hurt or destroy" the earth anymore (v. 25).

Red Letter Christians believe that Jesus Christ has already initiated this new Kingdom. Jesus told the people of His day that God was keeping His promises, and that there were signs of the coming Kingdom if they only had eyes to see. The Good News is that in Him, what Isaiah prophesied is even now breaking loose in history. The Kingdom of God is *transformed people living in a transformed society*, and when we preach this message to people in our day, we are preaching the gospel, the Good News. This hope for God's Kingdom on earth has been, since Christ, in the process of being actualized.

In present day Christendom, there has been a tendency to forget that both the salvation of individuals *and* the transformation of society are Kingdom non-negotiables. There are some Christians who act as though all that's needed to bring God's Kingdom is the transformation of individuals through traditional evangelism. Those who hold this point of view believe that if enough people are personally converted by coming into relationships with the living Christ, there will be no need to engage in social action programs or to get politically involved. *After all*, they reason, *won't a godly society naturally emerge if enough individuals are converted into Spirit-filled Christians? Won't godly people create a godly world? Isn't personal evangelism enough to facilitate Kingdom-building?*

There is much truth in the belief that "sacred" people produce a more just society. After all, it is through such transformed people, whom the Bible calls "the Church," that God is presently at work in the world, changing it into the world He wills for it to be. The Church, says Scripture, is the chosen means through which God will change the world. In Ephesians 1:21-23, we read:

> Far above all rule and authority and power and dominion, and above every name that is named, not only in this age but also in the age to come. And he has put all things under his feet and has made him the head over all things for the church, which is his body, the fullness of him who fills all in all.

God has chosen to use the Church to usher in the fullness of His presence in history, and the primary way through which the Church changes the world is by commissioning its members to serve in each and every social institution ("principalities and powers," see Eph. 3:10; 6:12) and, like leaven (see Matt. 13:33) and salt (see Matt. 5:13), to permeate these institutions with Kingdom values. Being in *all* the world, living out the love of God, working for justice whenever opportunities arise, and talking about how God is impacting their lives are the activities that make ordinary Christians into effective change agents, and together living the fullness of the presence of God.

One of the main reasons I became a Christian was that I was told I would be joining an army that was doing battle with evil forces, powers that were all too evident and often in control of the world around me. I was told that I would be joining with other Christians and participating with God in revolutionizing society. Such a calling whetted my appetite to do something heroic with my life! But once recruited, I was told that my assignment in the army was to be a recruiting sergeant whose duty was to recruit other recruiting sergeants who, in turn, would recruit other recruiters . . . and so on! It wasn't long before I had the sense that this "army" I had joined was not much more than a battalion of recruiters who were recruited to recruit recruiters, *ad infinitum*. I was led to believe that this was the only responsibility of Christians.

I couldn't help but ask an obvious question: *Where are the soldiers who are doing battle with the "principalities and powers" of this age? Where are the ones who, according to Ephesians 3:10, are supposed to bring all "rulers and authorities" into subjection to God's will?*

Some Christians choose to think that when the apostle Paul used the phrase "principalities and powers," he was referring only to demonic spirits. For those who hold to this belief, "spiritual warfare" consists in praying against these demons and resisting their evil powers in Christ's name. But biblical scholars point out that this phrase has a much broader meaning. Experts in biblical language, such as Dutch theologian Hendrik Berkhof, explain that "principalities and powers" in Paul's writings refer to *any* forces that transcend us and have significant influences on what we think and do. Consequently, while *including* demonic entities, these scholars contend that "principalities and powers" also refer to such suprahuman institutions and influences as the media, government, the educational system and the economic structures of society.[1]

If Paul, inspired by the Holy Spirit, was passing down a mandate to the Church, somewhere along the line there must be Christians who will engage the "principalities and powers" of our societal system to make something of God's justice evident within them. And that is where politics come in. It is by getting involved in political processes that Christians exercise one significant method of transforming society—so that within it, justice can roll down (see Amos 5:24).

There are three choices we must make if we are to have a biblical approach to political involvement.

Issues Over Party

I believe that Red Letter Christians should take their places as members in *all and any* political parties, both nationally and locally, that are both democratic and egalitarian. Their presence will act as the "leaven," permeating those political parties so that they increasingly promote the kind of justice and social well-being that actualizes the prophet Isaiah's vision of the Kingdom of God.

As Christians get involved in party politics, however, they must avoid the tendency to define *any* party as "the God party." Some Christians come close to believing that the principles of political conservatism are the will of God, and that any who hold to liberal political ideas are misled at best, and evil at worst. On the other hand, there are Christians, especially in academia, who act like condescending elitists who believe conservatives are unsophisticated bumpkins unacquainted with "what's really going on."

In reality, conservatives and liberals need each other: Conservatives maintain many lines that should never be crossed, while liberals destroy many lines that should never have existed.

Let history show that conservatives have held the line against those who would allow pornography and sexually destructive forms of behavior to pervade the nation. They have been the countervailing influence that has preserved the best of our free enterprise system against dangerous socialist tendencies, and they are the ones who have worked hard to ensure that non-sectarian religion remains a significant ingredient in public discourse.

But before conservatives get too proud about being the flying buttresses that have kept the great American traditions from collapsing, they should consider that liberals led the campaign to give women the right to vote, and were also the primary advocates for civil rights legislation. Liberals were the ones who challenged long-established racial and gender lines that had made many Americans into second-class citizens. Sadly, condemnations of Martin Luther King, Jr., and Nelson Mandela were far too common among conservative Evangelical leaders who, to their credit, think otherwise today.

On some issues, Red Letter Christians are conservative and on others we are liberal. Neither end of the political spectrum has a corner on the will of God.

Authority Over Power

One of the great philosophers of history, Arnold J. Toynbee, once said, "Those whom the gods would destroy, they first make drunk with power." As Christians take up membership in our various political parties, we must be careful, lest we be seduced into playing power games within these organizations. We must take care as we get involved in politics, lest we fall victim to power's destructiveness. There is a great temptation to play power games and organize into a voting bloc, or even perhaps to create our own separate political party. In gaining political power to put "our own people" into office, it would be all too easy to impose what we are convinced is God's will on the rest of society. This deceptively simple plan for creating God's Kingdom on earth is attractive, but ultimately counter-productive. Such power plays can do nothing but expose the arrogance that leads us to suggest that our views on issues and our solutions to society's problems are divinely inspired—that we speak for God.

Instead of using power to mold public policies, we should endeavor to speak with authority to those in power. The sociologist Max Weber gave classic definitions that differentiate *power* from *authority*. In *The Theory of Social and Economic Organization*, Weber explains that *power* entails the ability to coerce or to impose your will on others. Conversely, *authority* is having the legitimate right in the eyes of others to expect that proposals will be embraced and followed. If you are followed because others have no choice, you have power. If you are followed because others believe you have a legitimate claim to their allegiance, you have authority.[2]

One example of this brand of authority was mentioned in the previous chapter: abolitionist William Wilberforce, who often quoted from Scripture when he addressed the British Parliament on the topic of its slave trade. Over the span of 20 years, he spoke with biblical *authority*—and in the end it was this authority that overcame the vested economic interests and deep-seated prejudices of many of his fellow parliamentarians to finally end the trade in slaves throughout the British Empire.

It is important to stress that for Christians, authority comes from sacrificing to meet the needs of others. As the ultimate case in point, Jesus speaks as "one having authority" (Matt. 7:29). He does not coerce us into yielding to His will. Instead, we come to an awareness that He has a legitimate claim to our allegiance through His sacrifices for us—especially His sacrifice on the cross. The apostle Paul makes clear in Philippians 2:5-8 that Jesus rejected power as His means for changing the world into His Father's Kingdom:

> Let the same mind be in you that was in Christ Jesus,
> who, though he was in the form of God,
> did not regard equality with God
> as something to be exploited,
> but emptied himself,
> taking the form of a slave,
> being born in human likeness.
> And being found in human form,
> he humbled himself
> and became obedient to the point of death—
> even death on a cross.

Jesus' sacrifice on Calvary earned Him authority—Scripture goes on to say that because of this authority, every knee ought to bow before Him, yielding complete obedience (see Phil. 2:9-11). That Jesus abandoned the use of power in bringing salvation to the world should come as no surprise in light of the temptations He resisted. After Jesus spent 40 days in the wilderness, Satan came to Him and tried to convince Him to use power to gain a following, first by turning stones into bread for the hungry (see Matt. 4:3). Then Satan tempted Jesus to amaze the masses by jumping from one of the high towers of the Temple on Mt. Zion and floating safely to the ground (see Matt. 4:5-6). Finally, Satan tried to seduce Jesus by offering his own power to establish His Kingdom on earth—but Jesus refused to take over the world by coercing humanity to do His will (see Matt. 4:8-9). In each case, Jesus rebuked Satan by using the *authority* of Scripture. Instead of using power, Jesus chose to establish His Kingdom through sacrificial love. Through the cross, Jesus would draw all men and women unto Himself (see John 12:32), because *authority is earned through sacrifice.* When we consider Calvary, we realize that we are not our own—we have been bought with a price (see 1 Cor. 6:20). The sacrifice Jesus made for us on the cross deserves our souls, our lives, our all![3]

As an example of how loving sacrifice earns authority, I can point to the authority my mother had over me. When she spoke, I listened and obeyed. She did not have the power to make me obey—I was bigger and stronger than she was. Instead, I obeyed her because I felt that I owed her my respect and obedience, in light of all the loving sacrifices she had made on my behalf over the years. She spoke with authority!

I once heard Mother Teresa speak at a National Prayer Breakfast, which was attended by the U.S. president, the vice president and a host of other world leaders. She said things that many of those present did not want to hear, but everyone listened to her with great respect. She spoke strongly against abortion, even though those at the head table with her were overtly pro-choice. She spoke with authority, authority that had been earned through her sacrifices for the dying poor on the streets of Calcutta.

On another occasion, Mother Teresa spoke to a graduating class at Harvard University. Again she said things about sexual morality and the sacredness of life that ran counter to the beliefs of most in the audience. And again, the audience listened with respect—because she spoke with authority. I surmise that if push came to shove, most Catholics would more likely have listened to Mother Teresa, who gained authority through her sacrifices, than to the Pope—regardless of all the power he wields as the head of the Vatican State.

I contend that Christians will only have authority if they first serve the needs of others in sacrificial ways, especially the poor and oppressed. When those who hold power witness how Christians live out love—meeting the needs of others and binding up the wounds of those who have been left hurting on society's waysides—Christians will earn the authority to speak. When Christians sacrificially give of their time and resources to run soup kitchens for the hungry and provide shelters for the homeless, they gain the right to be heard. When they tutor poor children and care for those with AIDS, they expand their mandate to call for change. But before they speak, Christians must demonstrate God's love through sacrificial ministries. Sacrifice gives them the ability to be taken seriously by those who seem to be in control of political machines.

Several years ago while in the Dominican Republic, I spent a day following around a young doctor named Elias Santana. This special and wonderful doctor had all the credentials necessary to establish a lucrative medical practice for himself in the United States. Instead, Elias chose to live out a life of sacrifice for the poor people of his own country. He spent some time each week earning big fees by providing medical services to the rich who lived in Santo Domingo; then he took that money and spent it on medicine, which he offered for free to the poor. Sometimes Elias even flew to nearby Puerto Rico to perform surgery in order to secure more funds for his work in the impoverished barrios surrounding Santo Domingo.

I followed Elias one day as he made his rounds to the various clinics he and his friends had set up in the worst slums of the city. At the end of that day, when his medical work was done, he climbed on to the top of the pickup truck that served as his mobile pharmacy. Then from his perch on the truck, he called the people of the barrio to gather around so that he could preach the gospel to them.

Standing on the edge of the gathered crowd was a young man I recognized. His name was Juan Perez. Juan was an atheist leader of the Young Communist Association at the Autonoma University of the Dominican Republic and a prominent member of the powerful Socialist Party.

I made my way over to Juan and asked—in an almost mocking manner—"Do you realize what he is doing, Juan? He's preaching the gospel! The people are listening. Do you think he's going to win some converts today?"

Juan's answer was memorable. With an edge to his voice that conveyed both an air of resignation and great admiration, he responded, "What can I say? Elias Santana has earned the right to be heard!"

When Elias spoke, he spoke with authority, authority that was established through his sacrificial service to the needy of Santo Domingo. Following the example of Jesus, his sacrifices on behalf of the poor demanded that he be taken seriously, even by those critical of Christianity, even by a member of a very leftist political party.

In these examples, we recognize some ways in which Christians can speak truth to power without playing power games. From the likes of Mother Teresa and Elias Santana, we learn that as we enter party politics, we must carry with us a track record of service and sacrifice on behalf of "the least of those" who are in need; then when we speak, we will speak as ones who have authority. Through sacrificial service we will be taken seriously and given fair consideration—and we may even be able to sway those who disagree with us.

I'm sure there will be those who can point out the flaws and shortcomings of this approach to exercising leadership in politics, who say that what I'm advocating is naïve and unrealistic. My critics will say that in the real world of politics, it is power—with all of its coercive potential—that is workable and necessary. And I must admit that there is, in what is often called "servant leadership," something of power games in even the most noble effort to exercise authority. The truth is that we are seldom free from power plays, regardless how hard we try.

Nevertheless, in Jesus we have one who embodied the ultimate expression of authority and who perfectly modeled servant leadership; unquestionably, He is the "ideal type" toward which we should aspire. Those who doubt the efficacy of authority over power should take note that the Christ who rejected power in favor of sacrificial love will ultimately triumph over the principalities and powers of the political world. That passage from the second chapter of Philippians cited earlier goes on to say:

> Therefore God also highly exalted him
> and gave him the name
> that is above every name,
> so that at the name of Jesus
> every knee should bend,
> in heaven and on earth and under the earth,
> and every tongue should confess that Jesus Christ is Lord,
> to the glory of God the Father (vv. 9-11).

His lordship was created through sacrificial love, and by following His example we too can gain authority. Only through our sacrifice, as we seek to meet the needs of others, will we have the authority to challenge the "principalities and powers" that are the rulers of our age.

Knowledge Over Ignorance

There is one more important requirement for effective Christian political involvement that needs noting: We must be an informed constituency. Democracy requires an informed voting public, and Christians must pay special attention to this requirement.

To gain the authority to speak and then not have the knowledge to speak in a credible manner is to be rendered foolish. We are told in Scripture that our work is approved by God when we correctly handle knowledge and truth (see 2 Tim. 2:15). We are required to have a reason for the hope that lies within us (see 1 Pet. 3:15).

Blind patriotism is not a virtue. Christians, to the best of our abilities, must work hard to understand the various perspectives on the "hot" issues of the day, and be able to reflect on these issues intelligently and biblically. As we think through issues, we must be willing to rise above party allegiances and develop our political positions in accord with what we believe to be the will of God.

I am still amazed at how often Christians simply adhere to positions dictated by preachers from the pulpits of their churches or fall in line with what they hear on Christian radio and religious television shows. Each Christian must work out his or her own "salvation" on political issues (see Phil 2:12), listening to what is said on all sides and then making personal decisions. The last thing in the world I want for anyone reading this book is that he or she uncritically follow what I say on these pages as if my views on political issues are the final word on what Christians should think. What I hope is that the political statements that follow will stimulate thinking and—ideally—demonstrate how just one Christian endeavors to use a biblically based theology to inform his political thinking.

I do not propose that my perspectives should be considered definitively Christian, nor that differing views outlined by other thinking Christians should be ignored. None of us are above making errors in our political thinking, and I have been most certainly proven wrong on various issues. When I consider the ways in which my own opinions have changed over the years, I am well aware that neither I nor anyone else has the final word on how Christians should vote on the crucial issues that confront us at election time. At best, I hope that this book challenges the reader to develop his or her own perspectives, and encourages him or her to use biblically based critiques to examine the pros and cons of contemporary political debates. To these ends, I hope that what follows proves helpful.

With all my emphasis on individuals working out their personal positions on the pressing issues that are hot at election time, I do not want for any Red Letter Christian to ignore how the Church can help. As each of us works out what he or she believes, there should be a willingness to share conclusions with fellow believers. Christ, working through us, can provide checks and balances that keep us from making serious mistakes. The critiques we receive from those who love us in Christ, even if they do not cause us to back off from positions we have taken on certain issues, will sharpen our thinking and, in accordance with Scripture, help us to work out our reasons for the hope that is in us (see 1 Pet. 3:15).

THE GLOBAL ISSUES

SECTION TWO

CHAPTER 3

THE ENVIRONMENT

For Red Letter Christians, creation care is a very big issue. It is one of the issues that separate us from that sector of the Evangelical community that wants the political attention and activism of Christians to solely focus on the hot-button issues of abortion and gay marriage. Even if we do not always agree on what to do about these two concerns, don't think for one moment that Red Letter Christians take them lightly. Quite the opposite is true; we take them very seriously. But we also are convinced that if we are to approach politics biblically, we must broaden the agenda to include several other crucial concerns. High on that list is care for the environment.

I for one didn't need to see Al Gore's *An Inconvenient Truth* to be convinced that something must be done to address matters related to climate change and global warming. A visit I made to Africa a decade ago was more upsetting than anything I had previously read about our destruction of planet Earth. There, I talked with the head of a remote village in Senegal. I had gone with a camera crew to chronicle the desolation and suffering caused by a drought that was devastating that part of the world.

As the two of us stood together on the banks of the Senegal River, which separates Senegal from Mauritania, this tribal chief talked to me about how the drought had decimated the herds of goats that had sustained his people for many years. He described how almost all the young men of the village had left and gone to Dakar, the capital, in hopes of finding jobs, because raising goats for a living was no longer viable. Then he said something that took me by surprise. In measured reflection he declared, "My people know how to survive droughts. We have done it for hundreds of years. This is something else. The weather is changing!"

That tribal chief and village leader was no climatologist, but he knew something on a gut level. He knew that the weather patterns according to which his people had organized their lives for as long as they could remember had been disrupted, perhaps beyond restoring. He knew that the lives of his people would never be the same.

Evidence like this for the reality of climate change is everywhere, but there are a variety of possible explanations for the causes of it. Most of us are aware of the consequences stemming from the dramatic increase of carbon emissions in the atmosphere due to the burning of fossil fuels over the last century, but there are a number of lesser-acknowledged factors to be considered. For instance, little attention is given to the rapid destruction of the rain forests in the Amazon region of Brazil, which some scientists have referred to as "the lungs of the planet." Rain forests absorb carbon dioxide in exchange for oxygen and produce much of the moisture that becomes rain. But the demand for more and more hamburgers and the consequent necessity of making room to raise more and more beef cattle have resulted in the destruction of an area the size of a football field *every minute*—an area the size of Washington state is destroyed every year.[1] This leveling of the Amazon jungle is almost certainly a contributor to the kind of climate changes recognized by that Senegalese chieftain as he stood with me on the banks of a river that was close to drying up.

There is no question about whether or not the earth is warming up, but there are arguments over the causes of global warming. A minority of climatologists, such as Roger A. Pielke, Sr., a Senior Research Scientist at the University of Colorado (Boulder), says that the warming we are presently experiencing is part of a normal cycle of temperature change that can be expected over an extended period of time.[2] He and other conservative scientists are ready to admit that there is global warming, but they raise questions about how severe the problems associated with it will prove to be.

Carl Wunsch of Massachusetts Institute of Technology (MIT) is ready to postulate that sea levels will rise as a result of global warming, but he goes on to say that nobody knows by how much.[3] Robert Mendelson, economics and climate change expert at Yale University, actually postulates that global warming would be beneficial to the economy over the next century. "The United States will likely enjoy small benefits of between $14 and $23 billion a year. . . . Recent predictions of warming suggest . . . that impacts are likely to be beneficial in the U.S."[4]

Relatively few scientists contend that there is no need for an alarmist response to global warming. In my view, we should be reluctant to give credence to those who say we are only experiencing the warm side of a recurring cycle when more than 95 percent of the world's scientists have concluded otherwise.[5] Most scientists agree that we have a real problem on our hands.

The Business Block

Despite the avalanche of evidence, the Southern Baptist Convention hailed a report from a handful of scientists that raises questions about global warming. The voting delegates to the 2007 gathering of the convention in Fort Worth, Texas, passed a resolution that claims that "scientific evidence does not support computer models of catastrophic human-induced global warming."[6] The resolution was passed because it was decided that major steps to reduce greenhouse gases would unfairly impact the world's poorest people. Dealing with climate change would be costly to industry (the argument goes), because many developing nations are experiencing the growing pains of early industrialization and would have great difficulty absorbing the costs of providing technologies to control industrial waste.

But a United Nations Climate Change Impact Report released in April 2007 found that it is those in poverty who will suffer most if we don't begin to control emissions. "It is the poorest of the poor in the world, and this includes poor people even in prosperous societies, who are going to be the worst hit," said Rajendra Pachauri, chairman of the research committee that presented the findings.[7] That is because climate changes resulting from carbon emissions interfere with agricultural food production, and with a scarcity of food, the poor will be the foremost deprived. It is clear that if we are truly concerned about our world's most vulnerable citizens, we must begin to care more wisely for our common home.

A more nationalistic and profit-centered reasoning against emissions controls comes from advocates of *laissez faire* capitalism, who say that because the evidence for a global warming crisis is less than conclusive (to their minds), we ought to be careful about allowing government to interfere with private industry's business. They point out that the cost of taking the necessary steps to significantly cut carbon emissions would be great, and that cost would make it increasingly difficult for American industries to compete with China, our major competitor in the world market. Given the way these folks size up the situation, it is easy to understand why those who believe that "the business of America is business" would be leery of any attempts to put more environmental controls on American industries. But are we really ready to sacrifice the well-being of our children and grandchildren because we are unwilling to pay the price responsible ecology requires?

Even as we consider the economic costs of dealing with the environmental problems associated with advancing industrialization and what might result from our government taking the steps necessary to deal with these problems, we should recognize the economic benefits that could result from creative solutions to our present predicament. There are an array of new "green" businesses and industries that even now are being created to address the call for ecological responsibility. In Germany, a leader in environmental technology, there are tens of thousands of new jobs being created and a great deal of money being made by creating energy from alternatives to using fossil fuels.

Recently, while traveling in the north of that country, I saw countless numbers of wind-driven turbines that provide a significant proportion of the electricity needed to meet the needs of the German people. Many of those turbines are privately owned by investors who are earning significant dividends on their investment in wind energy. The jobs being created in the manufacturing and deployment of those wind turbines, along with the jobs essential for their maintenance, are serving as a boon to the German economy.[8]

There are also economic benefits to recycling, another green industry. Already here in the U.S., the recycling of paper, glass and steel reaps good profits for companies that were early to get into the business. And investors should realize that there will have to be more recycling in the future if Americans are going to avoid being buried under huge piles of all we throw away. For instance, outdated, discarded computers are piling up at an incredible rate, and the need to recycle them is reaching a critical stage. We also have to be concerned about large plastic toys like slides, swings and playhouses, which presently seem indestructible. Something can and must be done about them. These are incredibly lucrative opportunities for innovative start-ups! Not too long ago, there were those who said there was no way to recycle Styrofoam cups and plates . . . but scientists have found a way and investors are reaping the returns.

The list of ways to glean profits in the process of addressing environmental concerns goes on and on. Imagination and initiative are needed to make green industries more common, and we should support companies and political candidates who give evidence of both.

The Treaty Test

Whenever there is a discussion about global warming, there is likely to be mention of the Kyoto Protocol of 1997, which was supposed to take effect by 2008. This particular treaty commits the signers to work toward reducing carbon emissions to levels lower than in 1990. It offers poor countries funding to develop new technologies that would diminish environment pollution. It also establishes tough systems to monitor carbon emissions, and legally binding consequences for countries that fail to comply with the treaty's requirements. A scaled-down version was drawn up and finalized in Bonn, Germany, in 2002, and now requires only Russian ratification to have a sufficient number of signers to take effect.[9]

But the Kyoto Protocol of 1997 was dealt a severe blow in March 2001, when President Bush announced that his government would not sign it. The United States, which was responsible for 36 percent of all emissions in 1990, agreed to reduce emissions by only 7 percent during the period between 2008 and 2012.[10] That would not be enough according to treaty requirements.

The barrier to signing, first for Congress and then for President Bush, was that China had been given a moratorium on having to take action against its emissions. The Chinese had argued successfully that, in an effort to catch up with highly developed nations, they needed time to increase their industrial output without being hindered by the restraints on pollution that the 1997 Kyoto Treaty requires.[11] The position of the Bush Administration was that this moratorium gives the Chinese an unfair competitive advantage over signers of the Protocol for world trade. Other industrialized nations, such as the United Kingdom and Germany, signed anyway, and most environmentalists believe that our country should have done the same.

Related concerns over global warming were elevated during a 2007 meeting of G8 nations in Germany, in which most of the leaders signed an agreement to significantly cut back on the carbon emissions in their countries by the year 2050.[12] Many environmentalists were angered when President Bush did not sign the U.S. to this agreement. But before harsh judgment is passed on our president by Earth-loving Red Letter Christians, let's recognize that his decision may have long-term positive consequences for our cause.

The president wasn't willing to sign the agreement because China and India, two of the world's worst polluters, were not involved with or committed to it in any way. President Bush plans to meet with leaders of these two countries in the near future to discuss with them the problems related to carbon emissions, as well as what their nations are willing to do about being environmentally responsible.[13] Obviously, if President Bush had already committed our country, he would come to that meeting with very limited bargaining power. By *not* signing the agreement at the G8 meeting, our president may have put the U.S. in a position to get India and China to make important concessions to the world's call to reduce carbon emissions.

The debate about the 1997 Kyoto Protocol and other agreements with our global neighbors still goes on. It is important to find out how candidates in the next election stand with respect to signing the Protocol and similar treaties, and if they are willing to commit America to its obligations.

Other Planet Problems

While climate change is the dominant environmental concern these days, it is by no means the only one. There is alarm about the rate at which we are using up the earth's unrenewable resources. Some scientists at Harvard and MIT have provided clear evidence that it is only a matter of time before the earth's limited oil supply is exhausted.[14]

Even more threatening to our well-being, fresh water—which we have considered to be plentiful—is becoming increasingly scarce.[15]

Our rampant and ongoing destruction of countless species of plants, insects and animals is already having grave consequences. What most of us do not realize is that almost all the medicines we use to treat many common sicknesses are derived from plants and other organic sources.[16] As our devastation of the environment makes many plants extinct, we have to wonder how many cures for serious diseases are being wiped off the face of the earth. Perhaps we are even now destroying some species of plant in the Amazon in whose leaves or roots hides the cure for cancer.

People are becoming increasingly concerned about what we eat. Chemical fertilizers have contaminated everything from the lettuce in our salads to the water we drink.[17] The mercury content in fish due to industrial wastes has required that the government issue warnings from time to time to keep us from eating certain kinds of seafood.[18]

There are other dire concerns about industrial waste. In Camden, New Jersey, a study conducted by a group of my students showed that some schools in that city are constructed on dump sites that evidence high levels of radon—a chemical contaminant that affects indoor air quality—which poses significant health risks for the children in those schools.[19] Scientists continue to uncover connections between health problems and the pollution of the environment. Their findings have many of us wondering to what extent the dramatic increase in cancer in recent years is related to the stuff we've been dumping into our rivers and pumping into our air.

We have yet to figure out just how much of the radiation coming from our use of nuclear fission to generate electricity has to do not only with cancer, but also with a variety of other maladies—we do know that the tragic accident at the Russian reactor at Chernobyl has been directly linked to high levels of birth abnormalities and cancer in that part of

Russia.[20] Perhaps most alarmingly, nobody knows what to do with the waste being produced by these nuclear power plants. It will take centuries for the radiation levels from the waste to dissipate to a safe level, and finding a place to store it until then is extremely problematic. (Among the wilder solutions being proposed is that the nuclear waste be put into rockets and shot into outer space.[21])

What Does the Bible Say About All This?

It is easy to make a biblical case for being environmentalists. The most commonly cited passage of Scripture to that end comes from the opening chapter of Genesis, wherein God gives us the obligation to be stewards of creation (see Gen. 1:26-28). Theologians from John Calvin in the sixteenth century to Ron Sider today maintain that this particular passage is a mandate from God to commit ourselves to creation care.

Whenever I preach on the calling of Red Letter Christians to environmentalism, I quote from Romans 8:19-22:

> For the creation waits with eager longing for the revealing of the children of God; for the creation was subjected to futility, not of its own will but by the will of the one who subjected it, in hope that the creation itself will be set free from its bondage to decay and will obtain the freedom of the glory of the children of God. We know that the whole creation has been groaning in labor pains until now.

To me, this is a clear injunction that we who are imbued with the Holy Spirit should be drawn into a commitment to save the earth from degradation. All of creation, according to these verses, is waiting for us to rescue it from its fallen condition.

It has been said that the difference between a politician and a statesman is that the politician makes decisions with the next election in mind, but the statesman makes decisions with the next generation in mind. How candidates tackle the environmental issues that now confront us will determine whether they are politicians or statesmen and stateswomen. We need clear and detailed answers from them about their views and priorities regarding environmental questions. Whatever the extent of your commitment to safeguard God's creation, insist that your party and potential candidates speak with clarity and specifics about these important matters so that you can make an informed decision about their positions. The stakes for the future are too high to settle for anything less.

CHAPTER 4

THE WAR

It may very well be that war is the decisive issue that will determine the outcomes of elections for years to come.

There is a great divide among Christians when the Iraq War is discussed. Evangelicals, for the most part, are supportive of the president's policies, while the leadership of mainline denominations is more prone to oppose the U.S. invasion and occupation of Iraq. Official affirmations of President Bush's administration have marked such gatherings as the annual meeting of the Southern Baptist Convention. At the same time, more theologically liberal groups, such as the National Council of Churches, strongly condemn the president's propagation of the War. The executive leadership of every major Protestant denomination related to the National Council of Churches has gone on record as opposing the war in Iraq, while the Roman Catholic hierarchy has generally followed the Pope in standing against any militaristic solution to the Iraqi crisis.

It's not that religious leaders in this latter group are categorically opposed to all war; it's that this particular war does not meet the standards for what their theologians characterize as a "just war."

Just War

It was St. Augustine, in the fourth century, who provided the classical definition of Just War theory. What Augustine outlined on this matter was given further explanation and elaboration by sixteenth-century Protestant reformer John Calvin. In brief outline, they argued that a just war requires the following conditions:

1. The cause must be just (not mere conquest).
2. The war must be lawfully declared (no sneak attacks).
3. The war must be declared only after all other options have been tried and exhausted.
4. The war must have a reasonable chance of success.
5. The use of force must be proportionate to the desired ends (no intentional killing of civilians).
6. The good accomplished must outweigh the harm resulting from the war.[1]

Those who question calling the war in Iraq a "just war" argue that there was neither sufficient evidence to claim that America faced imminent danger at the hands of Saddam Hussein's regime, nor had all alternatives been exhausted to resolve the conflicts with Iraq. They further claim that the advice of people in the military was ignored in terms of what it would take to win the War and secure the peace, and that the War was undertaken without any realistic awareness of the damage that would be done to the Iraqi people.

Right now, still embroiled in the conflict, it is difficult to wade through the facts, much less the pros and cons for starting this war. There is a great deal of cynicism, and many conspiracy theories abound. Bill Moyers, in a PBS special series, has gone so far as to propose that there was intentional deception by the president's team—those who planned the War in the days leading up to its start. With the use of an extensive array of video clips, Moyers attempts to show how the president, the Secretary of State, the National Security Advisor, the Secretary of Defense and the vice president conspired over and over again to connect Saddam Hussein's government with Al-Qaeda. Moyers suggests that the Bush Administration employed an old propaganda tactic that says if an untruth is told often enough by those in authority, what is said will be believed—even if there is no evidence to support the claims. In reality, points out Moyers, there was absolutely no evidence that linked Saddam's Iraq with Al-Qaeda and the pilots who flew the airliners into the World Trade Center and the Pentagon on 9/11. Those pilots hailed from two countries *allied* with the United States: Egypt and Saudi Arabia![2] If Bill Moyers is to be believed, the ploy worked: Even now an overwhelming proportion of the American populace believes there was a connection between Saddam Hussein and the 9/11 attacks, and assumes that our invasion of Iraq was justified as a form of retaliation for what Saddam Hussein's regime did to us.[3]

If the facts and evidence do not support a clear declaration that our action in Iraq is a just war, the question for many critics of the Church is whether or not it was the responsibility of Church leaders to sound the alarm *before* military action. Should they have studied the evidence and, if they found it inadequate to justify the War, made what they discovered known to their congregations? Considering the high price of going to war based on unsubstantiated declarations from government leaders, was it not the responsibility of those who exercise prophetic ministries in the Church to challenge unsupported claims that would lead to extensive suffering and death? Where were the informed and courageous preachers when the drums of war began to beat? Where were the brave voices of those willing to take the risks that come with speaking truth to power?

Justifications for War

Of course, arguments can be made to justify the War, even if these justifications do not fall under the standards of Just War theory. The most common of these is that tyrants must be stopped before it is too late. The proponents claim, referring back to World War II, that if Hitler had been stopped sooner, tens of millions of lives could have been saved.

Those who continue to support the war in Iraq claim that our government leaders know many things that they cannot tell us "for security reasons." They say that we must trust what our elected officials tell us because those in high office would never lie to us about such matters—especially when those leaders have declared themselves to be born-again Christians.

But those leaders' justifications for the invasion of Iraq and for our continued occupation of that country have changed over the years. Initially we were told that the invasion was necessary because Saddam Hussein had developed weapons of mass destruction, which could be rained down on America and our Western allies within 45 minutes after launch.[4] When Secretary of State Colin Powell spoke at the United Nations and presented what were supposedly irrefutable proofs of those weapons' existence, most Americans rallied to support the War. According to one report, only 18 percent of Americans opposed the invasion.[5]

The president himself was convinced by the words of a top executive in the CIA, who held that the case for justifying an invasion on the basis of the Iraqis' having weapons of mass destruction was a "slam dunk."[6] Following the invasion, we learned, to our dismay—and I personally believe, to the dismay of President Bush—that such weapons were nowhere to be found.

I honestly do not think the president deliberately misled the American people. Unlike the cynics (and cynicism is an un-Christian trait), I choose to believe that, from the top executives in the White House down to citizens like you and me, everyone was misled by faulty reports from the so-called "intelligence community." There was bipartisan support for the War. Both George Bush and former President Clinton supported an invasion and viewed Saddam Hussein's powerful army as a threat to peace and stability in the Middle East—but I absolutely believe that neither wanted an *unnecessary* war.

When the weapons-of-mass-destruction rationale for the War was discredited, spin doctors in Washington then promoted the claim that the really important reason to occupy Iraq was to destroy a tyrannical regime and to establish a democracy there.[7] Sadly, that hope has not been realized. Following free elections, an Islamic Republic was established with Shi'ites in control of the government. In countries under Shi'a rule elsewhere in the world—such as Iran—the rights of women are curtailed and the religious freedoms of non-Muslims are severely limited. If a democracy is a society wherein the rights of minorities are protected, then Iraq is not a democracy.

The most recent justification for the War is the claim that this military action has been part of our ongoing "War on Terror." In the words of the president, "We have to fight them over there or else we'll have to fight them over here."[8] Those who point to the Iraq War as part of a larger struggle to protect us from terrorist attacks say that eliminating terrorists over there will keep terrorists from doing their evil deeds here on American soil.

There may be some logic to this line of thinking—and it must be acknowledged that as of the writing of this book, there has been no major terrorist assault within the United States since 9/11, which lends some credibility to the claim—but I myself am apt to challenge it. I propose that instead of diminishing the number of terrorists who threaten the well-being of our citizens, the war in Iraq has increased their number. As Iraqi civilian casualties range into the high hundreds each month, families of those casualties become embittered and, in their bitterness, become easy recruits for terrorist groups like Al-Qaeda. Prior to our invasion, there were no accounts of terrorists coming from Iraq, but now there is no doubt that Iraq has become a major breeding and training ground for terrorists.[9] I am reluctant to say it, but I believe that for years to come, the angry militant Iraqi terrorists created by this war will strike back at the U.S. and the nations of Europe in ways that will stagger the imagination.

You don't get rid of terrorism by killing terrorists any more than you get rid of malaria by killing mosquitoes. You get rid of malaria by getting rid of the swamps that breed mosquitoes—and you get rid of terrorism by eliminating the conditions that breed terrorists. Until we deal with the oppression of Arabs in places like Palestine and address the poverty that plagues so many people in the developing world, terrorists will continue to be recruited in growing numbers.

The Unfolding Aftermath

There is little doubt that support for the war in Iraq is evaporating by the day. Presently, the overwhelming proportion of the American electorate believes that the War was a mistake.[10] Sadly, the primary reason for this change of attitude is not the result of a growing awareness of the possible immorality of the War. Instead, it is due to images and stories from the media—whether true or not—that give the strong impression our side is losing. Social critics say that if we were winning the struggle, support for the War would be strong. America loves winners and is harsh on losers. What does this say about the moral grounds for our attitudes?

Some experts estimate that more than 300,000 Iraqi civilians have died as a result of this war.[11] That figure dwarfs the number of those who were massacred under Saddam Hussein. Entire cities have been devastated.

Basic services, such as electricity and clean water, continue to be in short supply.[12]

What many are calling a civil war between Sunni and Shi'ite Muslims has broken out.

Millions of people—including most of the professionals such as doctors, lawyers and teachers—have fled the country.[13]

The Iraqi economy is in shambles.[14]

In light of the horrifying conditions in Iraq, it becomes increasingly difficult to argue that removing the tyrannical, sadistic regime of Saddam Hussein has made life better for the Iraqi people. Add to that the thousands of American soldiers who have lost their lives, the many more thousands who have had life-crippling wounds, and the 24 percent of returning veterans who will require psychiatric care and psychological counseling,[15] and for many Americans, the price of the War now seems too high to pay.

Jesus once said that before a competent king goes to war, he takes stock of his army and resources and considers whether or not he has the wherewithal to win that war. If he is not sure, he tries to negotiate some kind of settlement (see Luke 14:31-32). It now seems obvious that our leaders failed to take stock of what would be required not only to win the war, but also to secure the peace. The results have been disastrous.

Worthy of consideration, but by no means of ultimate importance, has been the enormous financial cost of the war. Presently, the war costs $2 *billion* every three days, or $232,000 *a minute*.[16] That kind of money could be used to eliminate malaria and tuberculosis in Africa, and would go a long way toward eliminating Third World poverty and addressing the HIV/AIDS crisis. If it's national security that concerns us, it's wise to pay attention to what a general in the British army in Iraq asked me: "When will you Americans learn that your security is more dependent on the friends you make than in the armies that you deploy?" That general was—and is—absolutely right! We could make a lot of friends by meeting the needs of the poor and oppressed people of the world with the billions of dollars we continue to waste on this war.

Another consideration that ought not be ignored is the debts incurred by the Iraq War. They are so great that we have had to borrow money from Saudi Arabia and China. Think of the ramifications of that!

America is borrowing more than a billion dollars a week from the Peoples' Republic of China.[17] What will be the consequences for the U.S. of being in debt to our greatest economic competitor? No wonder we seem so weak when we come to the bargaining table with the Chinese; it's difficult to negotiate when those on the other side of the table are holding your bargaining chips.

The Mission's Impact on Missions

In the midst of our nation's conflicts with Islamic peoples, we should give careful consideration to what those military missions are doing to the evangelistic efforts of Christian missionaries in Muslim countries. The American invasion of Iraq has been reported regularly in Muslim countries as a rebirth of the horrors that Muslim peoples endured during the Crusades of the Middle Ages.[18] While those Crusades took place in the remote past in our Western minds, we must realize that our Muslim neighbors have much longer memories. What happened to them a thousand years ago is part of their consciousness today. Consequently, American soldiers are commonly referred to in Muslim propaganda as modern-day versions of the Medieval Crusaders. This has severely hampered the ability of our missionaries in various Muslim countries to do what they were called to do: win people to Christ.

In Baghdad, for the first time in centuries, churches have been burned down by Muslim extremists. There are reports that Christian women who have refused to adopt the dress prescribed by some Muslim sects have had acid thrown in their faces, and that threats against Christians have escalated so sharply that they are fleeing Iraq by the thousands. Where once there were more than a million Christians in Iraq, there are now less than 600,000.[19]

Every time I attend a missionary conference, I hear talk of reaching those who live in what is called "the 10/40 window" with the gospel. This particular region of the world reaches from 10 degrees above the equator to 40 degrees below the equator, and extends from the Atlantic to the Pacific across Africa and the Middle East. It is presently the least-evangelized area in the world. Only a minute minority of those who live in the 10/40 window have any idea who Jesus is and what He did for them through His death and resurrection. Most of those who live in this area are Muslims, and they *have* heard about what our armies are doing to their Muslim brothers and sisters in Iraq, and what the U.S.-backed Israeli troops are doing in Palestine. What they hear makes them increasingly unreceptive to the message of our missionaries about the love of Christ and the love of Christians. Some Christian missionaries to the 10/40 window have been martyred and many others have to endure ostracism and rejection.[20] I have heard one report that the number of missionaries in Pakistan has dropped from 400 to 40 as a consequence of recent events, but when I have tried to get exact figures on this exodus of missionaries, I've found it nearly impossible. What I do know is that the number of missionaries there has dropped dramatically.

George Verwer, the founder of Operation Mobilisation—one of the most effective and far-reaching missionary organizations in the world today—is one of the few Evangelical leaders who were aware of the possible negative effects of the War, long before our troops invaded Iraq. He worried about what his hundreds of young missionaries would have to face in the way of imprisonment and persecution once the War began.[21] But even with his sterling credentials as an Evangelical leader, Verwer was unable to convince his Evangelical brothers and sisters of the impending consequences of the War on the missionary enterprise of the Church.

The Growing Resistance

Among Red Letter Christians, there are a growing number who are either pacifists or non-violent resisters of war who make the claim that taking the words of Jesus in the Sermon on the Mount seriously bars His followers from warfare:

> You have heard that it was said, "You shall love your neighbor and hate your enemy." But I say to you, Love your enemies and pray for those who persecute you (Matt. 5:43-44).

I have a bumper sticker on my car that reads, "When Jesus said, 'Love your enemies,' He probably meant we shouldn't kill them." Even my pro-war Christian friends smile when they read it.

There are many supporters of the War who believe that the Sermon on the Mount was not meant to be lived out in our present age, but instead sets down for us the ethical standards that will be set in place when Jesus physically returns to bring His Kingdom on Earth. Most Red Letter Christians do not accept that assertion and believe that the Sermon on the Mount was meant to be lived out literally in the here and now.

During the Vietnam War, a young member of the Church of the Brethren (one of the Anabaptist peace denominations) was brought into court because of his refusal to be inducted into military service. As he made his case for not participating in what he believed was an unjust war, the judge was visibly moved. He was impressed by the obvious sincerity of the young war protester and filled with regret when it came time to hand down a sentence.

Sadly the judge said, "Son, in ruling on this case, and given the requirements of the law, I have no alternative but to . . ."

At that point, the young man interrupted the judge in a loud voice, "I have something to say!"

Again the judge tried to speak. In a solemn and regretful voice he said, "I have no choice but to sentence you to . . ."

Again the young man interrupted him, and this time went on to say, "You do have a choice, Judge! *You can resign!*"[22]

It is this kind of radical Christianity that is expressed and lived out by a growing minority of very committed Red Letter Christians. Even those of us who have serious questions about the realism of our pacifist brothers and sisters are beginning to understand their stance. I myself am very troubled by the extreme commitment of non-violent resisters because I realize that brave men and women have gone into battle—and many of them have died—in order to grant the privilege of taking a stand to those who are conscientious objectors. This is one of the things that makes America great!

Yet even with my personal dilemma over pacifism, I respect the position of my resister friends. In the face of war, their uncompromising commitment to Jesus' words is becoming increasingly attractive to the rest of the Christian community.

These idealists propose that we should deal with our enemies according to St. Paul's teaching in Romans 12:20, which reads:

> If your enemies are hungry, feed them; if they are thirsty, give them something to drink; for by doing this you will heap burning coals on their heads.

Some claim it is naïve and unrealistic to directly apply these directives of Scripture to situations in our highly complex world. But I'm not so sure! Suppose we had done just what the Bible tells us to do prior to engaging in this war? What might have been the results?

For 10 years before we invaded their country, the Iraqi people suffered because of a trade embargo that the U.S. promoted in hopes of turning the Iraqi people against Saddam Hussein. The embargo was set in place with the expectation that the deprived people would react by bringing down their evil dictator. It didn't happen! Saddam became ever more entrenched in power while, according to the Red Cross, as many as 500,000 Iraqi children died as a direct result of that embargo.[23]

Just suppose that we American Christians had used our vast financial resources to buy massive amounts of food and medicine, circumvented the embargo by shipping it all to Jordan, and then trucked it across the desert to meet the needs of suffering Iraqis. Might we not have brought down coals of fire on Hussein's head, just as the Bible says, and thus undermined his regime?

It's not that the Christian way of dealing with enemies has been tried in such international conflicts and then failed. It has not been tried—not really!

Getting Out

Whether Americans were for or against getting into this war, the main question we're all asking right now is how we can get our troops out of Iraq without leaving a disastrous situation behind.

Jesus once talked about how an unclean spirit was cast out of a man, but because nothing was brought in to replace that unclean spirit, seven worse unclean spirits came in to take its place (see Luke 11:24-26). That seems to be what has happened in Iraq. We cast out one demon (Saddam Hussein), only to create a vacuum that has sucked in other demons to take his place—insurgents, Iranian revolutionaries, Al-Qaeda and a host of warlords—all of whom have made things worse than before.

There is a near-total breakdown of law and order in Iraq.

Terrorists regularly set off bombs that blow innocent citizens to smithereens.

Sectarian warfare has devolved into what has all the hallmarks of a civil war.

Insurgent forces that are little more than gangs of thugs run rampant through the streets of the cities. Many Iraqi towns teeter on the verge of chaos.

Polls show that 70 percent of the Iraqi people want our troops to leave immediately.[24] One British general caused consternation among politicos in both Britain and the U.S. when he announced his contention that the presence of the Coalition troops was only aggravating the situation.[25] Shortly after his remarks, the Iraqi Parliament demanded that our government provide a timetable for the end of our military involvement.[26]

The question is how to do so without leaving behind a completely disorganized society, devoid of the social controls that make it possible for people to live in safety.

Recently, Rabbi Michael Lerner, a progressive Jewish theologian and editor of the magazine *Tikkun*, collaborated with me to propose a way to end America's military involvement in Iraq. We invited religious leaders from all faiths to sign on with our plan and then published it in a full-page ad in the *New York Times*. Here is what we proposed:

1. President Bush should go before the United Nations and confess that, based on reports from intelligence experts, he had believed that there were weapons of mass destruction in Iraq, and that is why he called for an invasion of that country. Those intelligence reports were wrong, and now hundreds of thousands of innocent people have been killed and entire cities were destroyed. For those sufferings and the deaths that have come about because of this invasion, the president should ask for forgiveness for himself and on behalf of the American people who overwhelmingly supported this great wrong.

There are those who will argue that such a confession would be a sign of weakness. I disagree! I believe it is a sign of spiritual strength and maturity to confess wrongdoing. Also, I believe that such a confession would go a long way toward restoring to America its stature as a moral nation, which has been diminished greatly because of the Iraq War. Those who think that the U.S. should never humble itself before the world ought to recall that oft-quoted Bible verse, "If my people who are called by my name humble themselves, pray, seek my face, and turn from their wicked ways, then I will hear from heaven, and will forgive their sin and heal their land" (2 Chron. 7:14).

2. We should call upon an international peace force to replace British and American soldiers. Such an international force would be composed primarily of Muslims from non-neighboring states, but include non-Muslims from other states not engaged in violence or economic boycotts against the Iraqi people. U.S. and British soldiers do not understand the language, the culture, or the religion of most Iraqis, and this has led to extensive misunderstanding.

3. Rebuild Iraq! True repentance requires deeds to back up the words. While this would require billions of dollars, it would cost far less than the continuation of the War—and would earn us some goodwill from the people of Iraq and from the rest of the world.[27]

We who signed this proposal really believe it will work. One thing is certain: "Staying the course" will only make matters worse.

As we consider for whom to vote, we must realize that it is not enough for candidates to condemn the War (as many Democrats have done) or to distance themselves from the president on the issue (as some Republicans have done). Candidates must be challenged to offer concrete proposals for what we as a nation should do in the days that lie ahead.

CHAPTER 5

PALESTINE

Few topics can generate more upset among Evangelicals than the politics and practices of the State of Israel—and no topic is more important for peace in the world than the politics and practices of the State of Israel.

Muslims around the world identify with the suffering of Palestinian Arabs. They consider what they perceive as America's tacit backing of Israel's actions against their Islamic brothers and sisters as justification for condemnation of both nations. Every day, extremist propaganda machines in the Muslim world grind out slanted and deceptively exaggerated reports of what Israelis are doing to the Palestinians who live in the Holy Land. As Muslims around the world read, watch and believe those reports, they cry out for justice for the Palestinians. Our government leaders cannot ignore their concerns. The perception in the Islamic world is that the power people in Washington determine whether or not there will be fair resolution for problems plaguing the Palestinian people—and the U.S. is held responsible for what happens in the Holy Land.

Our concerns for the Palestinian people should not keep us from trying to understand the crisis in the Holy Land from the average Israeli's point of view. The majority of Israeli Jews desperately want peace with their Arab neighbors, but they find it difficult to pursue when Arab rockets lobbed into their cities cause indiscriminate deaths, and when suicide bombers who kill their children are lauded as heroes among a large part of the Arab population.

The volatile situation in Palestine can be confusing, but Red Letter Christians must be informed about its complexities if we hope to be peacemakers (see Matt. 5:9).

A Short History Lesson

For more than 1,900 years, the primary victims of the Nazi Holocaust were a people of the Diaspora. When the Romans sacked Jerusalem, first-century Jews were left without a land to call home, and over time they settled in various countries around the world, especially in Europe. Wherever they went, Jews were forced to endure social discrimination and often deadly persecution.

Given what they endured as aliens in those nations and the anti-Semitism they faced from "Christians" everywhere, the birth of a Zionist movement—that saw a land of their own as the only hope for Jews to live in peace—is not surprising. Thus it was with incomparable joy that Jews throughout the world celebrated the decision by the United Nations to create a Jewish homeland. In 1947, Palestine was partitioned into Jewish, Arab and "international" areas, with the latter including Jerusalem and Bethlehem.[1]

There were, at that time, about 600,000 Jews living in the Holy Land and about 1.3 million Arabs, 10 to 15 percent of whom were Christians.[2] Palestinians objected to the fact that land on which they had been living for hundreds of years had been suddenly taken from them and given over to Jewish settlers, but with great joy, the Israelis accepted the 55 percent of the Holy Land assigned to them. In 1948, they declared it an independent nation. In reaction, surrounding Arab armies attacked Israel, but Israel prevailed.

During the war, more than 350 Palestinian villages were destroyed in the territory that was to become the State of Israel, and more than 600,000 Palestinians became refugees.[3] These refugees fled to Jordan, Lebanon, Syria and to those parts of Palestine known as the West Bank and the Gaza Strip.

In the intervening years, due to an ongoing flow of emigrant refugees and one of the highest birth rates in the world, the population in the West Bank and the Gaza Strip has grown to about 3.7 million.[4] These Arab peoples consider themselves imprisoned–Israel controls all movement in and out of these territories, not allowing the Palestinians to have an airport or seaport to serve as means for shipping and transport. Economic conditions in the Palestinian territories have deteriorated, creating extreme poverty and malnutrition, especially among children. It is awful, though not surprising, that the Palestinians have tried to strike back at their Israeli neighbors. Employing the worst kinds of terrorist techniques, they have wounded and killed many innocent Jewish civilians. Israeli Jews live in an ongoing environment of fear. Parents pray that their children can get to and from school without terrorist bombs tearing their buses apart.

The Arab peoples in the region provoked a war with Israel in 1967. In what has come to be called the Six Day War, the Israeli's won a decisive victory. This was possible largely because U.S. backing of Israel helped that small country to establish the fourth-most effective military in the world.[5] After the conflict, Israeli armies occupied lands that had been designated by the U.N. for the Palestinians, which included the Golan Heights, Gaza, the Sinai and the West Bank–including Jerusalem. Six months later, the U.N. Security Council passed Resolution 242, which condemned the acquisition of land by force and called upon Israel to withdraw from all occupied territory.[6] Israel did not comply.

Since 1967, there have been other wars in the Holy Land (such as the Yom Kippur War in 1973), additional calls for Israel to withdraw from occupied territory (such as U.N. Security Council Resolution 338), and continued defiance by Israel.[7]

Further aggravating the tense and explosive situation, thousands of Jews have moved into the illegally held territories. Over the years, the Israeli government has supported Jewish settlement in land that was originally granted to the Palestinians. By the year 2000, there were 225,000 settlers in 209 settlements in the occupied lands, in direct violation of international law.[8] That number has grown significantly since then. These settlements, which are now protected by thousands of Israeli troops, are a major barrier to any peace accord in the Middle East.

A more recent development that has the Palestinians beside themselves with anger is that since November 2005, the Israelis have been building a wall to separate Palestinians in the West Bank from territory claimed by Israel.[9] This wall is being built, ostensibly, to protect the Jewish population from terrorist attacks, especially from suicide bombers who might wander into their midst. In this respect, the wall has been a great success. Since its construction, the decline in terrorist acts in Israeli territories has been beyond anyone's expectation.

The problem, however, is that the Palestinians view the wall—and its twin separating Israel from the Gaza strip—as imprisoning them. The wall intrudes deeply into the West Bank to encompass Israeli settlements. In building it, the Israelis have taken increasingly more land away from the Palestinians. Furthermore, the wall divides several Palestinian villages and separates many families from their farm land. There are now more than 200,000 Palestinians on the Israeli side of the wall who are separated from the rest of their people.[10] (The enclosure of Bethlehem is a prime example: Part of the Mount of Olives, including the Garden of Gethsemane, is cut off from the rest.) Adding to the problem is that the barrier increases Israeli control of the region's fresh water supply, leaving an inadequate amount for the burgeoning Palestinian population.[11]

A Reason to Hope

In spite of all these problems, there is still reason to hope: An overwhelming majority of both the Palestinians and Israelis want peace.

That peace between Arabs and Jews is possible was evident when the leaders of Israel and Egypt agreed to sign the Camp David Accord in 1979. Both Egypt and Israel have kept the requisites of that treaty. Israel showed that it was willing to trade land for peace by withdrawing its troops from the Sinai and yielding sovereignty over that land to the Egyptians. Since then, polls show that the Jewish people, for the most part, are willing to trade land for peace, if there are assurances that the Palestinian government is ready to recognize the legitimacy of the State of Israel and stop the attacks by terrorists that have plagued them over the last half-century.[12] This is easier said than done—but it can be done.

In 2003, U.N. Secretary General Kofi Annan announced a "Roadmap to Peace," and President Bush has made this plan the cornerstone of his Middle East policies.[13] The settlement, agreed to by the United States, the United Nations, Russia and the European Union—and seemingly addressing the concerns of both Arabs and Jews—would, in compliance with United Nations resolutions, end the occupation of land taken from the Palestinians. It also would establish an independent, democratic Palestinian state and allow for a just solution to the Palestinian refugee problem to be negotiated at some future date. The Roadmap was accepted by the Palestinians and affirmed by the Arab League.

The Israeli government, on the other hand, said it would accept the Roadmap *only* if there were certain provisions included. These provisions would give them the right to control all entry and exit of persons and cargo by land, sea or air in and out of Palestine; control of Palestinian radio and television; and the waiver of any right of return to Israel of Palestinian refugees. They also insisted that all references to withdrawal of Israel from the occupied territories be removed from the Roadmap; that future negotiations for a Palestinian constitution and government be constructed in cooperation with Israel and subject to review; and that there be a cessation of any Palestinian military incitement against Israel without Israel committing to cease such incitement against the Palestinians.[14] These conditions have placed an indefinite hold on the Roadmap, and many observers believe that the plan is now stymied, if not dead. President Bush, however, has not given up on the Roadmap, and he should be given credit for his persistent efforts to work out agreements with both Arabs and Jews in order to make the plan viable.

Christian Zionism

A review of the difficulties the president faces may show that his biggest problems may not be those presented by either the Israelis or the Palestinians, but by those who have come to be called "Christian Zionists." This is a sizable group within the Evangelical community that believes that *all* the land God promised to Abraham, as found in Genesis 15:18, *must* belong to the Jews. Most of these Christian Zionists argue that having the entire Holy Land in the hands of Israel is required for the fulfillment of certain biblical prophecies, which they say lead up to the return of Christ. These particular Christians form a powerful voting bloc. President Bush cannot afford to ignore them, because they constitute a significant part of his political base.

As a case in point, consider the grief the Christian Zionists caused for both President Bush and Ariel Sharon, then Prime Minister of Israel, when Israel unilaterally withdrew its troops from the Gaza Strip in 2006. They were irate because land they believed God willed to be in the hands of Jews had been given back to Arabs. Evangelical talk radio all across the country claimed that Bush was acting contrary to the will of God by supporting Sharon's decision. Pat Robertson had to apologize for saying on one of his television shows that God was punishing Ariel Sharon with an incapacitating stroke for turning Gaza over to the Palestinian Authority.[15]

Christian Zionists fail to realize that a careful reading of the Bible gives Arabs, as well as Jews, the right to live in the Holy Land. The land in question was promised to the *descendants* of Abraham, and Arabs are also the descendants of Abraham. They are the progeny of Ishmael, whom Abraham fathered with his concubine Hagar (see Gen. 16).

Furthermore, the land that was promised stretches from the Euphrates to the Nile (see Gen. 15:18-21). Are Christian Zionists suggesting that all non-Jews be driven out of Lebanon, part of Syria and a big chunk of what is now Egypt? The more extremist Christian Zionists would probably say yes, and go on to assert that if those Arabs do not leave voluntarily with due compensation, they should be driven out by force. The ramifications of that kind of thinking are frightening, to say the least.

Listening to All Sides

Some of the Israeli conditions for accepting the Roadmap may not be as unreasonable as critics of Israel might at first suppose. For instance, the Israeli concerns about returning Palestinian refugees are valid. Consider the fact that, over the years, these refugee families have had such a high birthrate that if they were allowed to return to what is now the State of Israel, they would outnumber Jews and might vote them into subservience. What is more, the *jihadists* among the Palestinians are not likely to lay down their arms, given their commitment not to rest until they "drive the Jews into the sea," as the oft-repeated slogan goes. Since 1948, the Jews have had to be on the alert against Palestinian terrorists, so it is easy to understand their cautions when considering that stipulation of the Roadmap.

After all the arguments for and against the Roadmap to Peace are considered, however, it may still be the best hope for a Middle East settlement. Without a solution to the disagreement of Palestinian refugees and Israel over control of illegally held territory in the Holy Land, there can be no peace in the Middle East, nor any guarantees of safety for the Jews by the Muslim nations of the world.

In Europe, surveys show that Israel's policies toward the Palestinians are considered the most serious threat to world peace, exceeding in the minds of most Europeans even the threats posed by Iran and North

Korea.[16] The world knows that it is the U.S. backing of Israel that enables Israel to do what it does. Consider that almost one-third of all the monies our government gives away in foreign aid each year goes to the State of Israel, enabling Israel to maintain its military might.[17] It is not surprising, therefore, that anti-Israel sentiments translate easily into anti-American sentiments.

One last, but very important, consideration for Red Letter Christians as they ponder all that is going on in the Middle East: What is happening to the sizable part of the Arab population that is Christian? It is often assumed that all Arabs are Muslims, but such is not the case. Some estimate that as much as 15 percent of the Arab community in the Middle East is Christian.[18] It is hard to say how many Christians still live in the Holy Land, because so many of them have fled. At one time, there were tens of thousands of Christians in and around Bethlehem, but today only a comparative handful remain.[19] Arab Christians want to know why Christian Zionists, who have great influence with the U.S. government—and by extension with the Israeli government—so often seem oblivious to their plight.

As the election campaigns get underway, it is crucial for Red Letter Christians to listen to all sides involved in the Middle East conflict, to carefully consider what biblically prescribed justice requires, and then to probe each candidate to find out what he or she proposes as the solution to this central problem of our nation's foreign policies. If candidates for national office do not seem to be informed about both Arab and Jewish concerns, or are unwilling to give informed opinions about President Bush's Roadmap to Peace, we must consider whether or not they are fit for office.

The Middle East conflict transcends partisan politics, and any candidate who takes a clear stand on it is apt to anger significant numbers of potential voters. Consequently, in this issue we have a good test of the courage and moral fiber of the candidates. Don't let any of them get away with evasive or "puff" answers. Speaking boldly and clearly to the most important foreign policy issue of our time is a litmus test for the character of a candidate. We cannot endure the consequences of politicians who are not ready to enact a plan for peace in the Middle East.

CHAPTER 6

THE AIDS PANDEMIC

The AIDS crisis is seldom high on the agenda of U.S. politicians—there just aren't many votes to be gleaned by making AIDS a major concern in a campaign. Yet how we as a nation respond to this pandemic should be of crucial significance to those of us who claim to be Christians. We cannot push this issue off to the side, acting as though it's not very important.

More than 40 million people are HIV-positive, and this may be a low estimate[1]—we know next to nothing about what is going on in the People's Republic of China, where the disease is running rampant. In Africa, where some 35 million known cases of the virus have been reported (as of 2005),[2] there are 12 million children who have lost one or both parents to AIDS.[3] The enormous death toll is almost incomprehensible.

DIVINE JUDGMENT?

Church people were initially somewhat reluctant to respond to the AIDS crisis because when AIDS first surfaced in New York City in the early 1980s, it was regarded as a disease of the gay community. Some Christian leaders had the audacity to declare that AIDS was some kind of special judgment God was bringing down on homosexuals for behavior they declared was "an abomination in the eyes of God!"[4] I have often wondered what kind of God those who make such judgments actually worship: Do they really believe that *they* are less deserving of God's wrath than those they condemn?

Today things have changed, and AIDS is contracted and spread predominantly through heterosexual relations. Infected women are often innocent victims who got the disease from their husbands, who contracted the virus via extra-marital affairs.

In Jesus' day, there was a disease regarded in much the same way as some Christians now regard the AIDS virus. Back then, lepers were condemned as abominable people whose disease was a punishment inflicted on those who were defiled in the eyes of God. But Jesus treated those untouchables who had leprosy as beloved children of His Father, and He ministered to them in ways that brought them help and healing. He *touched* lepers, which, according to the laws of Israel, should have rendered Him "unclean" (see Lev. 22:4-7). But Jesus brushed aside such laws and the attitudes they embodied, and He let it be known that lepers were loved by and infinitely precious to His heavenly Father.

I believe that Jesus would do the same thing for those suffering from AIDS in our world. I also believe that He would again rebuke those segments of the religious community who attribute such diseases as leprosy (now called Hansen's disease) and AIDS to some extreme form of God's judgment on those who commit especially deplorable sins.

Divine Opportunity

In a *Christianity Today* interview in 2002, Bono, AIDS activist and lead singer of the Irish rock band U2, said, "We will be judged by this moment, by God and by history . . . if the church doesn't respond to this, it will be made irrelevant."[5] I couldn't agree more. God is calling us, for the sake of His Kingdom, to respond.

It is disturbing to realize that our government has failed, for political reasons, to provide the kind of help needed to address the AIDS crisis, specifically the rapid spread of the virus in Africa. To his credit, President George W. Bush has worked hard to increase funding for programs to combat AIDS, but Congress—especially those in his own party—have failed to give him the backing he needs.[6] Too often, these elected representatives want the money President Bush has requested for the AIDS crisis to be used for programs in their own districts—because bringing home federal money helps increase their re-election chances. Sadly, many of their pet projects have been "boondoggle" programs that have done little to serve the nation's good.[7]

Red Letter Christians must call on candidates to declare themselves on this issue and, when elected, hold them to any promises they made to support the struggle against AIDS. We must increase our sensitivity and concern for AIDS victims in Africa and in other developing parts of the world. At election time, we should require candidates to tell us if they are willing to commit our government to providing the kind of help needed to deal with this dreaded disease, giving special attention to the needs of the world's poorest citizens.

Most people in developing countries do not have the means to buy anti-retrovirals (also referred to as ARVs), which can retard the progression of AIDS in those infected.[8] Our legislators should be urged to put restraints on pharmaceutical companies that have obscenely overpriced these drugs, making them inaccessible to most of the world's poor. The public relations directors and press agents of such pharmaceutical companies will undoubtedly argue that their companies are compelled to charge such high prices for ARV medicines due to the high cost connected with their research and development. But these spokespersons do not bother to mention to us that we, the taxpayers, significantly contribute to that research with our tax dollars.[9]

In addition to lacking needed medical services, the poor of the world almost always lack the educational programs required to keep AIDS from spreading. Because of a lack of information and the spread of misinformation, many do not even know that AIDS is spread through sexual contact. Unbelievable as it seems, in some places it is believed that AIDS is some kind of CIA plot to wipe out racial groups that America deems undesirable![10] In the developing world, those infected seldom have the kind of counseling services that explain how to care for themselves so as to slow the progression of the disease. AIDS victims need to know what diets are most advantageous and what precautions should be taken to avoid passing on HIV.

There is one matter related to the AIDS crisis on which some of our most prominent Christian leaders have taken a reprehensible stand: making condoms available to needy people in developing countries. Some of these leaders, who have enormous influence on tens of millions of voters throughout the country, have demanded that the availability of condoms *not* be part of any programs our government sponsors.[11] Those who oppose distributing condoms argue that to do so is to encourage promiscuity. Given the political clout of these Christian leaders, politicians have been prone to capitulate to their demands—and the results have been horrendous.

Refusal to make condoms available to the poor in developing countries has contributed to an increase in the number of cases of AIDS in several countries where previously there was evidence that the spread of AIDS was near to being brought under control.[12] Reflective of the attitude of those who would withhold condoms is a report of an emotional confrontation between the CEO of a large faith-based relief organization and one of these anti-condom leaders. The prominent leader had learned that as part of its AIDS program, this particular relief agency had been making condoms available to young African women. He announced that he would tell those who listened to his radio programs to end any financial support they might be providing to the organization.

The CEO of the agency begged the well-known Evangelical, who had access to a huge array of supporters, not to do it. "Imagine," he said, "a 17-year-old girl who is the sole support for her younger brother and sister, and whose only means of earning the money she uses to feed and keep them alive is to prostitute herself. What would *you* do for her?"

The Christian leader replied, "Well, I wouldn't give her a condom!"

"But, what *would* you do for her?" asked the head of the agency again.

And again the man retorted, with great emotional intensity, "Well, I wouldn't give her a condom!"[13]

There are other Christians who argue in favor of making condoms available, claiming that it is one of the primary means for saving the lives of many innocent people. As has been already suggested, many women have become infected with the AIDS virus through no fault of their own because their husbands have been promiscuous—often with prostitutes. These men bring home the virus and then infect their wives, who unknowingly pass the virus on to the unborn they carry or to infant children through breastfeeding. The vast majority of all AIDS victims in Africa are such women and children.

A few years ago, I was one of the speakers at a large conference of African church leaders that met in Pretoria, South Africa. The speaker just before me had preached a powerful sermon, which neither he nor I thought to be cross-culturally insensitive. But we later learned that it was. He had said, "We all realize that if the people of Africa were surrendered to Christ and lived according to biblically prescribed morality, this AIDS crisis would not exist!"

His words had seemed so obviously true to me and beyond question. The crowd, however, was outraged—they knew that the overwhelming proportion of those Africans who are HIV-infected are women and children who in no way have violated biblical standards for sexual behavior.[14]

The American evangelist who made these unfortunate comments left for home shortly after his sermon and was not aware of the controversy that followed his preaching. The upset among those at the conference, however, was so great that the president of South Africa, who happened to be in attendance, used his authority to connect with the airplane carrying the evangelist and arranged for him to apologize to the conference via radio connection.

Mother Teresa once said, "Whenever I look into the eyes of a person dying of AIDS, I have this eerie sensation that Jesus is staring back at me."

Would that all of us would regard those with AIDS in such a manner. Bono has pled with America—especially with American Christians—to see this crisis as an incredible opportunity to show the people of Africa and the rest of the world what caring people we are. Would that we would seize this opportunity and demand that those who would be our country's elected leaders do the same.

THE HOT-BUTTON ISSUES

SECTION THREE

CHAPTER 7

GAY RIGHTS

Seldom have social issues generated as much concern as over the issue of gay marriage during the 2004 election. Karl Rove, one of the most effective campaign strategists in the Republican Party, made sure that referendums on gay marriage were placed on the ballots of key "swing" states, knowing that the emotion generated by this issue would bring out the Evangelical vote—and it did![1] Political scientists are agreed that this issue may have been the deciding factor that carried the state of Ohio for the Republicans and won the election for George W. Bush.[2]

Voices on religious radio and television almost universally condemn gay marriage and urge their listeners to vote against it. These powerful voices, usually from the Religious Right, often claim that gays and lesbians can change their sexual orientation if they really want to. They preach that to allow gay marriage, or even civil unions between homosexual partners, is to encourage willful disobedience to God's will as revealed in Scripture.

Along with a whole lot of shouting and condemnatory preaching about the matter, there is a great lack of knowledge on the subject. The truth is, nobody really knows the causes of homosexual orientation. We do know that nearly all scientific studies on the subject have found that same-sex attraction is not chosen.[3] Furthermore, there is a growing body of knowledge to suggest that there may be multiple causal factors involved,[4] and many experts suggest that the causes for men and the causes for women may be very different.[5] There is also widespread acceptance in the scientific community of the claim that the homosexual orientation is established so early in childhood that gay people have no remembrance of ever being other than they are.[6]

Most of those who counsel gays and lesbians are agreed that there is almost no chance for them to change their sexual orientations, and whatever rare possibilities may exist are more weighted toward lesbians changing than gay men.[7] Even the leaders of Exodus International, a network of Christian ministries created to help gays and lesbians deal with their struggles, are now saying that homosexual tendencies will be evident during the entire lifetimes of those who reject same-gender sexual involvement and opt for heterosexual marriage.[8]

Given these generally accepted realities, there are a host of divergent opinions as to how the Christian community should respond to gays and lesbians. Sadly, many voters—and especially Christians—fail to take time to talk and listen to gays and lesbians to hear about their concerns and struggles. It's amazing how many extreme conservatives on the issues of gay marriage and gay rights change how they think and feel when members of their immediate families "come out" as homosexuals and they make time to listen to their stories. I think that if more people did so, the inflammatory rhetoric from both sides would die down and we'd begin to dialogue effectively.

Gay and Straight Rights

When it comes to public policy, we must ask whether the religious convictions of some should determine the rights and privileges of those who do not hold the same beliefs. As more people have considered this question, there have been tendencies in favor of gay marriages over the last decade.[9] (However, the latest study by the Pew Research Center shows that there may be a reversal of this trend in the immediate future.[10]) It may be that the issue of homosexual marriage will not figure as prominently in the upcoming election as those on the political Right think it will—there is growing evidence that the American people are tired of talking about it, and that their attitudes are changing.[11]

While there is still consensus that most Americans don't like gay and lesbian couples having their relationships called "marriage," for the most part they support the proposal of civil unions.[12]

Most people recognize that one of the principles that gave birth to our nation is that there should be no taxation without representation. With that in mind, most people agree when it is asserted by homosexual-rights groups that if gays and lesbians pay taxes, they should have all the same rights as the rest of us. Right now, gay couples are denied some of these basic rights, which include:

- Partners being denied Social Security benefits
- The refusal of auto insurance companies in some states to cover same-sex couples
- Prohibitions in some communities against gay couples having joint ownership of homes and businesses
- Denial of food stamps and low-cost housing for gay couples who are poor
- Denial of benefits for the partners of gay veterans
- Denial by hospitals in many states of a same-sex partner's visitation rights or access to the ill partner's medical records
- The option of some state courts to set aside the will of a homosexual person so that his or her partner does not receive an intended inheritance
- Denial of the privilege to file joint tax returns

The U.S. Government Accountability Office cites 1,138 rights enjoyed by heterosexual couples that presently are denied to homosexual couples.[13] The rest of us are largely unaware of how the system discriminates against gays and lesbians and do not understand why they are pressing for equal rights. One gay man I know told me that if we believe there should be no taxation without representation, then we should tell homosexual people that they don't have to pay taxes as long as they are denied equal representation under the law. "If you offered us that," he said, "you'd have the biggest coming-out party in history." I agree. Given that kind of proposal, I think a lot of heterosexuals would raise their hands and yell, "I'm gay! I'm gay!"

Of special concern is the "Don't Ask, Don't Tell" policy of the U.S. military. Almost 10,000 young men and women have been thrown out of the American armed forces since this policy was put in place.[14] Many of those discharged are among the few who spoke Arabic, Kurdish and other Middle Eastern languages, desperately needed translators in Iraq. In a *New York Times* Op-Ed piece published on January 2, 2007, John M. Shalikashvili, chairman of the Joint Chiefs of Staff when the policy was enacted, wrote, "With evidence that has emerged over the last 14 years, I now believe that if gay men and lesbians served openly in the United States military, they would not undermine the efficiency of the armed forces." He noted that a new Zogby poll of more than 500 service members returning from Afghanistan and Iraq found that three-quarters of them said they were comfortable interacting with gay people. He also noted that "24 foreign nations, including Israel, Great Britain and other allies in the fight against terrorism, let gays serve openly, with none reporting morale or recruitment problems."[15]

Gay and Straight Marriage

There are those who argue that making homosexual marriage legal would undermine the marital institution, and that the already weakened American family would be pushed further toward total collapse. To those who say that homosexual marriages would exercise destructive influences on traditional marriages, there is the counter argument that it may do just the opposite, in fact strengthening traditional marriages.

Advocates for gay marriage claim that what they propose communicates that they value lifetime commitments, are against promiscuity and believe marriage is a good thing for families and society as a whole.

Of course, there is no way to predict anything about what might be the consequences of gay marriage in the foreseeable future, but I believe, given the evidence, that any future collapse of the nuclear family would not result primarily from gays and lesbians getting married. I like to point out that when it comes to preserving marriages, we should focus on heterosexuals. Heterosexuals are the ones getting divorces—gays want to get married!

To prove that the institution of marriage is in trouble requires no extensive sociological study. It's a well-known fact that the divorce rate hovers near the 50-percent mark for all marriages performed in a given year,[16] and that as many as 20 percent of couples in America live together without being married.[17] This is all the evidence needed to make the point. But to suggest that prohibiting homosexual marriage is a major step in the direction of strengthening the institution of marriage is a far stretch. If we are sincere about preserving marriage as an institution, let's start with efforts to deal with the divorce problem in America, and ask ourselves how we can make traditional heterosexual marriages more satisfying and stable.

President Bush has come out strong against gay marriage, although he has not voiced opposition to civil unions for homosexual couples. He has said that marriage is a sacred institution and should be reserved for the union of one man and one woman.[18] If this is the case—and most Americans agree with him on this—I have to ask why the government is involved at all in marrying people. If marriage really is a *sacred* institution, then why is the government controlling it, in a nation that affirms separation of church and state?

Personally, as a Baptist minister, I always feel a bit uneasy at the end of the weddings I perform when I have to say, "And now, by the authority given unto me by the Commonwealth of Pennsylvania, I pronounce you husband and wife." At weddings, after having performed a variety of religious exercises, such as reading Scripture, saying prayers, giving a biblically based homily and pronouncing blessings on the marriage, I suddenly shift to being an agent of the state. Doesn't it seem inconsistent that in a highly religious ceremony I should have to turn the church into a place where government business is conducted? Isn't it a conflict for me to unify my pastoral role with that of an agent of the state?

Allow me to suggest a way out of this conflict and the difficult questions being raised these days about whether our country should approve of homosexual marriages. I propose that the government should get out of the business of marrying people and, instead, only give legal status to *civil unions*. The government should do this for both gay couples and straight couples, and leave *marriage* in the hands of the Church and other religious entities. That's the way it works in Holland: If a couple wants to be united in the eyes of the law, whether gay or straight, they go down to city hall and legally register, securing all the rights and privileges a couple has under Dutch law. Then, if the couple wants their relationship blessed—to be *married*—they go to a church, synagogue or other house of worship.[19]

Marriage should be viewed as an institution ordained by God and should be out of the control of the state. Of course, homosexual couples could go to churches that welcome and affirm gay marriage and get their unions blessed there, but isn't that the way it should be in a nation that guarantees people the right to promote religion according to their personal convictions? If such a proposal became normative, those like myself who hold to traditional beliefs about marriage would go to traditional churches where conservative beliefs about marriage are upheld, and we would have our marriages blessed there. And secularists who are unlikely to do anything that smacks of religion would probably just throw a party to celebrate a new union. Marriage would be preserved as a religious institution for all of us who want to view it as such, and nobody's personal convictions about this highly charged issue would have to be compromised.

It is not likely that this will happen in the near future, but many sociologists tell us that America is eventually headed toward making this the way we do marriage.[20]

In upcoming elections, it might be wise to probe candidates about what they think of this proposal, if for no other reason than to explore whether they are open to innovative solutions or if they simply speak from a fixed, ideological position.

Hate and Discrimination

Following the horrible murder of Matthew Shepard in Wyoming in 1998, there was an outcry for federal legislation that would provide for the prosecution of crimes against homosexuals motivated by hate. Some states known for their more liberal politics have enacted such laws. However, many politically conservative Christians argue that current laws are more than adequate to deal with any injustices that gays and lesbians might have to endure. "After all," point out conservatives, "those who killed Shepard were brought to justice, and no additional laws passed down by the federal government were needed to prosecute the murderers."

The whole discussion about whether or not special civil rights laws should be passed to protect gays and lesbians takes me back to the 1950s and 1960s, when parallel arguments, both pro and con, were made for whether or not African-Americans and other minority groups needed special laws to protect them from discrimination and physical harm. In some Southern communities in those days, racial prejudice ran so high that even if the evidence clearly pointed to white persons committing crimes against black persons, it was highly unusual for a white jury to hand down a conviction. But after federal civil rights legislation was passed, those who had committed crimes (including murder) and been let off because of racially biased juries could still be prosecuted in federal courts on the grounds that the civil rights of victims had been violated.

The question is raised by some gay rights advocates about whether or not there are counties in America where there is such hostility against homosexuals that juries might fail to pass guilty verdicts on persons who do harm to gays and lesbians. They point to evidence that certain judges have passed shockingly lighter sentences on guilty offenders when their victims were homosexual.[21] These activists argue that homosexual people today need the kind of laws that were passed a generation ago to prosecute racist crimes, giving them the same federal recourse if juries and judges in local communities have governed their decisions by anti-gay attitudes.

The major complaint against the passage of federal hate-crime legislation is that in some way such a law might hinder preachers from sharing their convictions about homosexuality from the pulpit. Christian pro-family groups from across the country have rallied on the steps of the U.S. Capitol to protest Senate bill 1105 and House bill 1592, which are similar proposals that would expand hate-crime categories to include sexual minorities and would make it easier for the federal government to prosecute hate-motivated violence against homosexuals. Having listened to the concerns of these protestors, I looked into the matter and found that this legislation carefully protects freedom of speech from the pulpit. Specifically, it states:

> Nothing in this act . . . shall be construed to prohibit any expressive conduct protected from legal prohibition by, or any activities protected by the free speech or free exercises clauses of the First Amendment of the Constitution (HR-1592, Section 8).

Nowhere in the bill is anything made into criminal behavior that is not already against the law.

What is often cited by those who believe otherwise is that when the bill was being debated on the floor of the House of Representatives, a question was asked regarding whether or not a minister would be legally protected if he preached a sermon on the Bible's teachings about homosexuality and then one of his parishioners went out and committed a hate crime. To this question, Arthur Davis, a congressman from Alabama, answered, "No."[22] What was going through Davis's mind is hard to say, but it's a stretch to contend that the incorrect answer of one congressman out of the 435 members of the House of Representatives constitutes a strong claim that the bill is designed to keep a preacher from preaching what he believes.

Having talked to several gay Christians about the need for hate-crime laws to protect homosexuals, I have received mixed responses. But I have discovered a unified opinion that federal civil rights legislation is desperately needed to protect gay, lesbian, bisexual and transgendered people from discrimination based on sexual orientation. That an early Republican candidate for the presidency responded to a question in one of the debates by stating that he would support an employer who fired an employee if he or she was discovered to be homosexual sent chills up many gay and lesbian spines.[23] There is also a fear among many homosexual people that they could be evicted from their apartments or rental homes if their landlords discover they are gay.

Given these kinds of fears and the realities of the world we live in, I join the homosexual activists in their efforts to establish legal protection against discrimination on the basis of sexual orientation. They, on the other hand, generally agree with me that exceptions should be made for churches and faith-based organizations. This exception is already built into pending legislation.[24]

There are extremists at both ends of the religio-political continuum who seek to manipulate voters with their alarmist messages. The author of a book entitled *Perfect Enemies*, Chris Bull, makes a convincing case that extremists on the Religious Right and the leaders of some left-wing gay groups, such as Queer Nation, raise money and recruit new supporters for their groups by painting outlandish scenarios of what could happen in our nation should the other side win the political struggle over gay rights.[25]

It is very important for Red Letter Christians to demonstrate some sophistication about the issues of gay marriage and gay rights by sorting through agenda-driven rhetoric to find a just way of resolving the political clash. We must wade through the extremist messages and deconstruct the inflammatory language heard from both sides, all of which distorts the truth.

Justice for gays and lesbians should be on the political front burner for Red Letter Christians on election day because it is impossible to tell people we love them if we deny them the basic rights we enjoy. And loving people—*all* people—is clearly preached in the red letters of the Bible (see Matt. 22:37-39).

CHAPTER 8

GUN CONTROL

One of the measures of a politician's courage is whether or not he or she is willing to make unambiguous statements about what should be done about guns.

There are huge political risks, regardless what stand is taken on gun control. Gun advocates are so well-organized and so well-financed that they can go a long way toward bringing down any candidate who crosses them.[1] On the other hand, politicians know that any poll of American voters shows that most of us want stricter laws curbing who can own guns and the kind of guns that can be sold on the open market.[2]

Generally, politicians make statements on this matter with so many caveats and qualifications that it's difficult to nail down their positions. Even if we could pinpoint politicians' views on gun control, however, Red Letter Christians are still left with having to establish *our* position. And for some, that is easier said than done.

To bolster their stance, Evangelical gun advocates usually point to Luke 22:36, when Jesus told His followers that, in anticipation of what lay ahead, each should buy a sword. Yet immediately following that command, we read that when Judas and the Roman soldiers came to arrest Jesus and His disciples made moves to do battle with their swords, Jesus told them not to do so—when one of Jesus' companions cut off the ear of the high priest's servant, He healed the wounded man (see Luke 22:49-52). Then Jesus said that those who "take the sword will perish by the sword" (see Matt. 26:52).

Pardon the pun, but you can see how Jesus' words can cut both ways.

I wish I could quote some verses of Scripture that clearly define a Christian position on this issue, but I can't. The best I can do is appeal to the calling of all Christians to seek what creates a safe and secure society. Given that calling—and even though many other Christians think otherwise—I am a proponent of stricter controls on who can own guns, on how guns can be purchased, and on what types of guns are available for sale. After listening carefully to many arguments from both sides of this controversial matter, I have a deep conviction that if Jesus were still physically incarnated among us today, He would not be packing a .40 caliber semi-automatic weapon. Having stated my bias, let's consider this volatile issue.

Federal Law

Any attempt to put restraints on gun ownership is greeted by pro-gun enthusiasts with the outcry that limiting guns in any way is a violation of the Constitution—and our very freedom is at stake! These are usually vague and unsubstantiated declarations by members of the National Rifle Association (NRA) stating that "citizens have the right to bear arms" without restraint. But most who make this claim have not bothered to read the Second Amendment to the Constitution, nor do they have a clear idea what it really says. For the record, the Second Amendment reads:

> A well-regulated militia being necessary to the security of a free State, the right of the People to keep and bear arms shall not be infringed.

As you can probably recognize, this amendment was designed to ensure the rights of individual states to maintain a militia so that their citizens could stand up to any totalitarian military threat posed by the federal government, or against other outside threats. Of course, there have been interpretations of the Second Amendment by the courts that have validated individuals' rights to bear arms.[3] But it should be noted, say gun-control advocates, that this reading is only *one* way the amendment has been interpreted, and it in no way can be read to prohibit the federal government from tightening gun laws in America or from regulating what individual states do about controlling guns.[4] Furthermore, the Second Amendment does not prohibit individual states from passing gun-control laws in order to improve public safety.

Since 1970, more Americans have been killed by privately owned firearms than the combined number of deaths in all the wars in U.S. history.[5] Americans have a reputation around the world for being violent and—if that stereotype is true, as the statistics indicate—I submit that it's probably not a good idea to put 200 million guns in their hands[6] without knowing exactly who among them owns those firearms.

State Laws

Individual states are where the real power lies when it comes to making laws to govern who can own guns and to govern the conditions under which guns can be purchased. And some of the laws established by states have serious loopholes. As hard as it may be to believe, many states actually have few (if any) controls on who can buy guns and what kinds of guns can be sold privately or purchased at gun shows. It is estimated that at least half the firearms sold at gun shows (about 25,000 a year) are sold without any background checks on customers and without any waiting period.[7] There is so little regulation that guidebooks for Al-Qaeda operatives suggest gun shows as the best places to get guns for terrorist activities.[8]

A very serious loophole was made public after the infamous Virginia Tech massacre in April 2007, when it was discovered how Seung-Hui Cho had purchased the guns he used to kill 33 people, including himself. This mentally disturbed young man had bought guns illegally, though it appeared that he'd purchased them according to established regulations. The error was due to a difference between how the federal laws define a disqualifying mental illness and how the Commonwealth of Virginia's laws defined it.[9]

Laws are never perfect, but almost any attempt to change or improve on poor laws is heavily resisted by the powerful gun lobby. Loopholes remain unclosed because the members of the National Rifle Association and other gun lobbyists want it that way.

Moral Law

In my view, there are too many Americans who are addicted to guns, or at least too many who are single-minded about their "right" to own them. Gun advocates claim that they are decent law-abiding citizens who should be allowed to own all the guns they want, if for no other reason than to protect themselves against the crazies of the world. They claim that the only real protection against the wrong people using guns is for the right people to have them readily available. "If some of those students in the classrooms of Virginia Tech had been carrying guns," they argue, "perhaps Seung-Hui Cho would not have been able to kill unchecked for more than two hours."

Gun ownership is a right that many Christians who are part of the Religious Right have held sacred for a variety of reasons. There is a strong belief among many of these politically conservative Evangelicals that we are living in "the last days" and that the forces of the anti-Christ are even now mobilizing for the coming warfare against God's people. In the face of this threat, the claim is made that Christians had better be armed and ready to stand against the forces of evil.

Many Evangelical gun advocates also suggest that there should be a constant vigil by heavily armed Christians against any threat of a militant takeover of America, possibly by those who advocate left-wing ideologies. These folks' strong commitment to rugged individualism leads them to believe that every person should be equipped to defend oneself, regardless of what protection the police or the U.S. armed forces might provide.

Making the case for stricter gun laws are people like Marian Wright Edelman, president of the Children's Defense Fund. She points out that every day, eight children and teenagers are killed with guns.[10] When it comes to youngsters dying from gun violence in America, *every four days* sees an equivalent to the Virginia Tech massacre.

Gun advocates would come back with the declaration that "guns don't kill people; people kill people." My retort is, Tell that to the loved ones of a six-year-old girl shot by a fellow classmate in Flint, Michigan. I doubt very much that the six-year-old boy would have killed her in school that day if he'd been holding a pencil instead of a gun.

A study done by the Harvard School of Public Health showed that accidental deaths from firearms among youngsters 5 to 14 years old are 16 times more likely to occur in the five states with the highest rates of gun ownership.[11] In those same states, children and teenagers are seven times more likely to commit suicide.[12] Those statistics don't *prove* anything—but they certainly suggest a great deal.

The police in cities such as New York and Philadelphia want the sale of assault weapons to be declared illegal. They claim that criminals they encounter in firefights often have law enforcement outgunned by more powerful and rapid-fire weapons. In some cases, the criminals' guns are even able to pierce body armor. These police departments also believe that there would be less gun violence if there were stricter laws controlling guns in general, more thorough background checks on buyers, and longer waiting periods between the time buyers complete the paperwork to purchase a gun and when they can actually get them.

In Philadelphia, the police commissioner pressed Pennsylvania state lawmakers to set up a separate system of gun control for the city that would allow the rest of the state to continue with the present system. He did not want to interfere with rural Pennsylvanians who enjoy hunting by forcing them to give up any of their gun rights. But the gun lobbies stepped in and nixed his efforts to reduce gun violence in a city that saw an almost 8-percent increase in its already high murder rate from 2005 to 2006.[13]

Tragically, it often takes a national catastrophe to allow gun-control advocates any success in fighting gun lobbies and laws. After President Ronald Reagan was seriously wounded in an assassination attempt in 1981, his press secretary, James Brady—who was paralyzed for life by the same attack—pressed to pass what came to be called the "Brady Bill." The Brady Bill mandates a five-day waiting period for purchasers who wish to buy some of the most extreme forms of weaponry—attack weapons with rapid automatic firing capabilities are specifically named in the bill. (The bad news is that politically conservative Democrats and Republicans who support pro-gun groups have been able to chip away at this important legislation over the last few years.)

For upcoming elections, consider whether or not legislation similar to—or even stronger than—the Brady Bill should be endorsed by a candidate seeking your vote. This is a pertinent consideration not only on the federal level, but even more so for state elections.

The National Rifle Association is one of the most powerful lobbies in national and local politics, and their members invest heavily in the campaigns of candidates willing to do their bidding. To stand up to the gun lobbies at election time is too much of a risk for most candidates. Even Democratic politicians—who do not typically give in to gun lobbyists as frequently as Republicans—can be highly influenced by the NRA during elections. Few things in the 2004 presidential race were more artificial and awkward than John Kerry taking time off from his campaign to get into full sportsman regalia and go duck hunting. It was rather obvious that he did so to curry favor with gun owners and pro-gun activists.

Generally I try to be evenhanded when dealing with hot-button political issues, but as you can see, I lose any sense of equilibrium when it comes to gun control. I am really upset with the pro-gun lobbyists! Please remember that I'm not saying we should abolish all rights to privately owned guns—I'm saying that we need to stop giving in to gun lobbies so that reasonable gun control laws can be made and enforced. As Red Letter Christians, let's ask the Holy Spirit to help us abandon any misguided notions we have about the use of guns; then we can begin to seriously discern what is reasonable and right when it comes to this very grave issue.

CHAPTER 9

EDUCATION

In many communities across the country, American schools are failing. Our students are falling behind those in other developed industrial nations. We are not providing sufficient numbers of graduates qualified to serve the needs of our technological economy.

Even more important, our educational system is failing to create citizens capable of understanding our globalized world and the issues confronting the U.S. at election time. Our government was founded on the premise that its voters would be properly informed to make political decisions. When our education system fails, democracy fails.

All Schools Are Not Created Equal

Of all the issues that ought to be considered regarding education, the one that deserves special attention from Red Letter Christians is the way in which education is funded in most states. Generally, financing for public education comes from local real estate taxes. This means that wealthy townships and boroughs with high-priced property have tax revenues that enable them to finance quality education, while poorer communities are left without robust funding to properly educate their children. All too often, the present system hurts the poor.

A case in point: In Radnor Township, Pennsylvania, where Eastern University is located, $15,526 a year per child is spent on education. Eight miles away, across the city line in Philadelphia, $10,635 a year per student is allotted for education.[1] That means that a classroom of 20 students in the rich township of Radnor has $200,000 more per year than does a classroom located in the inner city of Philadelphia. Making matters worse, most urban schools need more services for their students than do most suburban and rural schools. City children are more likely to come from troubled homes where there is often little encouragement for their education, and city schools often need more staff to do extra counseling and to handle a heavier load of disciplinary cases.

While many claim that the problems of our educational systems cannot be solved by throwing more money at them, few would fail to acknowledge that money can make a difference.

My friend David Hornbeck, one-time superintendent of the Philadelphia school system, once begged the state legislature of Pennsylvania for supplementary funding to add to the meager financial resources available through city real estate taxes. He argued that such additional funding would enable him to bring the students in the city's schools up to the same level of academic achievement as those who attended the better schools in surrounding suburban communities. The state legislators, most of whom came from the more affluent suburban and rural voting districts, voted against Dr. Hornbeck's funding proposal, to keep their constituents from paying higher taxes. Instead, they approved a mere 10 percent of the amount Dr. Hornbeck had proposed.

The superintendent decided, rather than spreading out this very limited additional funding over the hundreds of schools in the Philadelphia School District, that he would spend it on 10 randomly selected city schools. Within just a few years, the academic achievement levels of the students in those 10 schools far exceeded those of other schools in the district, and outstripped even the academic accomplishments of students at some of the elite schools in the Philadelphia suburbs.[2]

Biblical justice requires that we address this inequity. One possible solution to the problem of unfair funding for schools has already been adopted by the State of New Jersey: The state legislature has established a minimum amount that must be spent per child, regardless where a child lives. If township property taxes cannot meet that minimum, additional funding from the state is provided. This solution does not create full equity between rich and poor school districts, but it does give every child in the state basic support for an adequate education.

When considering a candidate, Red Letter Christians should ask about how that candidate would handle the problems of educational funding for the poor. If the response evidences a disregard for the needs of poorer school children, remember what Jesus said about anyone who offends a child: "It would be better for him if a millstone were hung around his neck, and he were thrown into the sea, than that he should offend one of these little ones" (Luke 17:2, *NKJV*).

I don't want to convey that inequities in the funding of education are the only reasons that children in poor urban neighborhoods are inadequately educated. Too often, inner-city schools waste money on superfluous administrative overhead. Incompetent teachers, protected by unions, must also be acknowledged as major factors contributing to academic failures. Furthermore, fiscal corruption and crony-ism, which are too often realities in our cities, result in wasted resources.

On both local and state levels, it is important for Red Letter Christians to struggle against the "principalities and powers" that determine educational policies and practices when those policies and practices do harm to poor children. In Camden, New Jersey, a city of 80,000 just across the Delaware River from Philadelphia, the level of fiscal malfeasance has been so great that at least a fifth of the money allotted for education has been lost. So corrupt and inefficient has been the Camden school system that the state board of education, via a decision made by the state legislature, was directed to take over the district, removing it from city control.[3]

I also don't want to give credence to the myth that inner-city school children are the only ones who are victimized by inadequate funding for education resulting from meager property taxes. In reality, half of the nation's poor live in impoverished *rural* areas where the schools lack adequate means for educating their children.[4] Because they get little media attention, the rural poor are often invisible to the general public.

There are still other factors that need to be considered when dealing with funding for education. For instance, there is a tendency among senior citizens to vote against any referendum that increases their property taxes. In communities where there is a disproportionate number of elderly people, this can mean less funding available for education. Many older people are on fixed incomes, and they sometimes view increased spending on education as a threat to their own economic well-being. When this is the case, the Church should step in to speak to elderly people about the need to be generous in looking out for children. The biblical imperatives to care for the young are clear, and preachers who are Red Letter Christians must make these obligations clear to senior citizens in their congregations. Red Letter Christians are not simply to vote in their own interests, but rather, to reject selfishness and vote in accordance with what serves the common good—especially the children of the poor.

To Voucher or Not to Voucher

Those who run Catholic parochial schools have long advocated vouchers for educational purposes, and Protestant Christians have recently joined Catholics in the crusade, hoping to gain public financial support for the increasing number of private Protestant schools. The voucher system is an arrangement whereby the parents or guardians of a child are provided with a certificate that is good for a specified amount of money, to be used for educating the child. These vouchers can be used to help cover tuition at private or parochial schools.

There are many valid pros and cons regarding the use of vouchers. The advocates of the system argue that it makes schools competitive. This drives schools to higher and higher levels of academic achievement as they compete against one another for students. Any school that isn't doing a good job would not likely be chosen by parents and soon would be out of business. Applying the principles of *laissez faire* economy to the educational system, some say, will ensure that people get a bigger bang for their tax dollars than is the case with our present system.

In a now-famous test case of vouchers in the Milwaukee school system, the results of this system have been very positive. Those children who took advantage of vouchers and went to private and parochial schools did much better academically than those who went to public institutions.[5] However, David Hornbeck, one-time superintendent of schools in Philadelphia, has empirical evidence that shows when traditional public schools are adequately funded, students do as well or even better than the vouchered students in Milwaukee.[6]

Another argument for vouchers commonly made by Evangelical Christians is that the public school system has been seduced into secular humanism. In many school districts, they point out, the slightest hint of religion is ferreted out and extinguished. They cite rulings by the Supreme Court that ended school-sponsored prayer and Bible reading in public schools as evidence of a secularizing trend.[7] Beyond that, there are reasons to believe that in some situations, children are being taught values that run contrary to what most Evangelical Christians believe and affirm. These Christians often point to sex education classes in which abstinence prior to marriage is not promoted and where certain homosexual lifestyles are taught as legitimate.

Some Evangelicals who believe in creationism are upset that their beliefs about the origins of humans and when and how the world was created are not given fair consideration. They do not so much object to

Charles Darwin's theories being taught as much as they protest the ignoring of their own views. They would like to see a public school system that is open to theories constructed on their convictions about a Creator. In most school districts, there are prohibitions against teaching the theory of Intelligent Design, which postulates that the universe was created over millions of years, guided by a trans-human intelligence. The elimination of theories that go beyond the paradigms of empirical science is upsetting to many Evangelical Christians, who believe that their explanation of creation does not necessarily contradict scientific evidence. They ask, "Shouldn't our theories be taught, if for no other reason than that tens of millions of Americans believe in them? Shouldn't the views of so many believers be respected? Shouldn't schools be open to variant, widely accepted points of view?" Because many public schools do not allow their views on creation to be considered in science classes, this presents some Evangelicals cause to promote vouchers. They want the means to send their children to schools that make room for their beliefs.

Such concerns over the propagation of a secular worldview have pushed many churches and other faith-based organizations into starting their own schools, in order to educate their children in an environment where their particular beliefs and practices will be respected.

Over and against those who argue for vouchers is an array of other Christians who are critical of them. The most common argument is that vouchers could end up destroying public schools because they drain financial resources away from public education. What is worse, say those opposed to vouchers, is that vouchers take monies away from schools attended by some of America's most socially disinherited children. They point out that there are a host of parents with children in poor schools who lack the kind of concern for their children that would lead them to take advantage of the voucher system and choose better schools. It is time, say opponents, to transcend political correctness and face the fact that a huge subculture has emerged in America, nurtured by such social forces as the media, with its rap music, MTV and glorification of a drug-centered way of life. In this subculture, there are all too many parents who have little concern for what happens to their children.

Consider the statistics about Camden, New Jersey, related in chapter 1. It's politically correct to say that all parents in that kind of place love their children as much as any other parents do—but a disproportionate percentage of them don't! The number of boys and girls in America who are left to fend for themselves is far beyond what most of us imagine, and we have to realize that school may be the only hope for children from such an environment. Would a voucher system result in such disadvantaged children being left behind, dumped into underfunded schools with poor facilities and discouraged teachers? This is a question that cannot be ignored.

Often racism contributes to advocacy against vouchers. There is little doubt that in the 1950s and early '60s, when segregated education was declared unconstitutional and bussing was initiated to ensure racial integration of public schools, many churches, especially in the South, established "Christian" schools to avoid "racial mixing." Most Christian educators these days recognize the evil of such racially offensive—and patently un-Christian—practices, and many have gone out of their way to provide scholarship help for poor families, and have even made special efforts to recruit "children of color." Unfortunately, however, not to acknowledge that there are still parents who would use vouchers as a means to minimize the involvement of their children with those of other races would be extremely naïve. When future generations look back on our society and condemn its racism, will they note the ways in which some Christians used the voucher system to promote segregation?

Still another argument from critics of vouchers stems from the fear that the public school system could become a magnet for students whom private, parochial and charter schools consider undesirable. It is much more expensive to provide for children with special needs. A disproportionate number of those who are physically and mentally challenged would possibly be turned away from private schools and end up in abundance in public schools due to the cost of educating those students. And would public schools, at the same time, because of the voucher system, have greatly diminished financial resources to deal with special-needs children?

And what about troublemakers? Private and parochial schools can expel them—and they usually do! Will our public schools become the primary places for those disciplinary cases that make teaching difficult for educators?

When Horace Mann, the foremost promoter of U.S. public education in the nineteenth century, laid out his reasons for a publicly funded system, he did so in the hope that such schools would promote the great "melting pot" phenomenon. Mann saw that America was a nation of immigrants, and he believed that a public school system was the best instrument through which children from various cultural backgrounds and with differing social values could be brought together into one culture, made up of individuals with common commitments.[8]

Will the fusing of Americans into a unified society with shared values be circumvented if public education goes into decline because of the voucher system? Will children from differing religious backgrounds be encouraged in religious and ethnic prejudices if they never interact in public schools with children from other backgrounds?

Several years ago, I was invited to be the speaker at a special prayer breakfast in Northern Ireland. The breakfast was on the morning of the initiation of peace talks aimed at moving toward some kind of reconciliation between Catholics and Protestants, and at creating a government wherein these two warring communities of faith could share power and responsibility for their common future.

I was seated at the head table. On one side of me was a bishop of the Catholic Church, and on my other side sat a prominent Protestant leader. Wanting to be as relevant as possible to the situation, I asked each of these religious leaders, "If there were just one thing that could change in Northern Ireland that would foster better relations between Catholics and Protestants and diminish religious prejudice, what would it be?"

Both of those church leaders responded that the best change would be an end to the separate schooling of Irish children. Because Northern Ireland had a structure similar to the voucher system, Catholic children and Protestant children had gone to separate schools for generations. In the separateness of their daily lives, the prejudices those children picked up at home were reinforced, with little chance of challenge.

Given what I learned that morning, I wondered what prejudices might be exacerbated by means of a voucher system here in the U.S. if increasing numbers of children are educated in religiously segregated schools. Would Black Muslims, who already have their own private schools, get funding from taxpayers to expand *their* educational system, and would this system, in turn, promote prejudice toward white people and special animosity toward Jewish people? And how long would it be before white supremacist groups such as the Ku Klux Klan and the Aryan Nation had access to tax dollars to finance schools that taught values that contradict the essence of what America should be about?

Leave No Child Behind

There is one more issue sure to come up when educational policies are discussed in upcoming elections that very much requires Red Letter Christians' careful attention: whether or not the No Child Left Behind Act, signed into law by President Bush in 2002, should be continued, modified or repealed. This law makes federal funding available to public schools contingent on how well students in those schools do on tests that assess their reading, writing and math skills and their comprehension of basic knowledge. Each year students in schools across the country are tested, and those schools in which the students fail to meet prescribed government standards lose some of their federal funding. On the other hand, those schools in which students do well are given increases in federal funds.

Some Democrats have sarcastically remarked that Bush's educational program should be renamed "Leave No Rich Child Left Behind"! When the Act was first explained in the African-American church where I hold my membership, I overheard one older woman remark, "Don't tell me Bush doesn't read the Bible! He must love that verse where it says that to those who have shall be given; and to those who have not shall be taken away even that which they have!" (see Matt. 25:29).

Some teachers complain that this program actually interferes with what they believe the educational process should be about: Instead of concentrating on helping students to think for themselves and explore their world, teachers' primary task in the classroom must now be to ready their students to take tests. Even worse, in some cases cheating is encouraged in a desperate effort to get additional federal funds. In Camden, New Jersey, a scandal was exposed wherein teachers felt justified in carrying out a variety of deceptions, promoting extensive cheating so that the test results of their students would be higher. When caught, these teachers said that they did what they had to do to get the federal funding that was essential for their schools.[9]

Whatever arguments can be leveled against the No Child Left Behind initiative, there is empirical evidence that the program has produced some notable improvements in the achievement levels of students across the country. In a comprehensive study made by *USA Today*, the Bush program got high marks.[10] Now, even some Democrats reluctantly acknowledge that the program is working to produce good results.

Candidates in upcoming elections should be asked about their plans for Bush's educational program, and Red Letter Christians should look for answers that transcend partisan politics and political ideologies. Democratic candidates often receive campaign funding from teachers' unions and the National Educational Association, which have been highly critical of No Child Left Behind. Consequently, they should be examined as to how funding from such special-interest groups has determined their positions, and to how they respond to the empirical data that supports the program. Those Republican candidates who support the president's program should be asked how it might be modified so as to overcome any justified criticisms.

As has been shown even in this limited discussion on the subject, there are a host of educational issues that Red Letter Christians should consider when they go into voting booths. To be informed on these issues is not only a requirement for good citizenship; it is absolutely essential for anyone who seeks to live out the message of Jesus in the red letters of the Bible.

CHAPTER 10

ABORTION

Abortion is, for many Christians, a defining political issue. It is so important to many Christian voters that it's not uncommon to hear, "Even though on all other issues I might be in harmony with a candidate, if that candidate is wrong on this issue, he or she won't get my vote!"

It was the abortion issue that sounded a wake-up call for Fundamentalists and got them politically involved. Through the greater part of the twentieth century, Fundamentalists remained politically dormant. Preachers who addressed political issues from their pulpits were accused of being "social gospelers" who had lost sight of the real mission of the Church: to save lost souls.

Everything changed with the Roe v. Wade decision of the Supreme Court in 1973, a decision that was a call to arms for Fundamentalist TV evangelists such as Jerry Falwell and Pat Robertson. Falwell led the way with the organization of the Moral Majority. With expert communication skills and superb networking abilities, he soon had millions of followers and hundreds of thousands of members in the movement. By 1980, he had mobilized enough support to say without any exaggeration that he delivered the votes necessary to elect Ronald Reagan to the U.S. presidency.

In the years that followed, Pat Robertson joined Falwell as a major political player and became another banner carrier for the pro-life movement. And he ran with it very effectively, actually running for president in 1988. At first, Robertson's candidacy was demeaned by the media pundits, but after he won second place in the Iowa caucuses, they had to take him seriously.

While Robertson's run for the presidency ultimately failed, he came out of his campaign with a nationwide grassroots political organization from which he—utilizing the brilliant strategizing skills of Ralph Reed, onetime leader of the Young Republicans—created the Christian Coalition. The Christian Coalition became one of the most effective political blocs in American history. Over the last two decades, this bloc of voters has gotten endorsed candidates elected to U.S. Congress, to state legislatures and to a host of local community offices.

Neither the Moral Majority nor the Christian Coalition (which have come, with similar groups, to be known collectively as the Religious Right) would have arisen had it not been for the legalization of abortion. This one issue was the hot button for Evangelicals that generated political involvement such as has seldom been seen in our nation's history. One of my friends wryly remarked to me, "All during the 1960s you were crying, 'All power to the people!' In the 1980s you found out who the people were."

Initially, the Republican Party couldn't have been more thrilled with the way the abortion issue swept millions of new members into its camp. Yet some of the old-line Republicans, whose commitments were primarily to the pro-business contingent of the GOP, quickly lost their enthusiasm for the marriage of their party with pro-life Evangelicals. The tensions between the Religious Right and what some call "the country club Republicans" have become increasingly evident through the years: The old guard often resents the agenda of the Religious Right and prefers to be free from the overt Christian emphasis they strive to impose on the party. Unfortunately for these more traditional party members, little can be done at the present time to free the GOP from its dependence on the Religious Right and its pro-life emphasis.

The Seamless Garment

Red Letter Christians are overwhelmingly pro-life, even though we refuse to get caught up in the power-centered politics of the Religious Right. Indeed, we initially adopted the name "Red Letter Christians" primarily to distinguish ourselves from right-wing Evangelicals. Most Red Letter Christians are unwilling to become single-issue voters whose politics are determined solely by abortion.

We readily admit that there can be times when one particular issue is so overriding in its importance that how a candidate stands on that issue should determine how we vote. Slavery during the nineteenth century was such an issue; there are some who say the same about abortion today. They maintain that if the unborn are to be regarded as sacred persons created in the image of God, then the hundreds of thousands of abortions performed each year must be regarded as a holocaust.

Common among Red Letter Christians is the belief that we should be *consistently* pro-life, which means that life is sacred and should be protected not only for the unborn *but also for the born*. This requires that there be commitments to stop wars, end capital punishment and provide universal healthcare for all of our citizens—in addition to stopping abortions. This consistently pro-life position was promoted by the late Cardinal Joseph Bernardin of the Catholic Diocese of Chicago, who referred to it as "The Seamless Garment," a reference to the garment Jesus wore (see John 19:23).[1]

The common ground for those who make abortion a defining political issue and those who do not is found in a willingness to work together to reduce the number of abortions.

In a recent study by the Guttmacher Institute, there is evidence that if Medicaid coverage included contraception for low-income women, as many as 200,000 abortions could be prevented each year.[2] According to this study, if the government also provided medical coverage for pregnant women who cannot afford doctor and hospital care, as well as daycare assistance for mothers who are gainfully employed to support themselves and their children, the number of abortions per year could be cut even more dramatically.[3] Too many low-income women, especially those who might become single mothers, cannot afford the necessities that so many of us take for granted.

Other proposals to decrease the annual abortion rate include guaranteed maternity leave so that women do not have to choose between job security and motherhood, and raising the minimum wage—studies show that a woman working full-time at the present minimum wage cannot afford the rent of even a low-cost apartment.[4] Another proposal deserving consideration is to establish special programs that allow young mothers to stay in school and complete their educations. Without a high school education, an unwed mother is likely to end up living well below the poverty line. Enabling poor women to afford a better life is an obvious way to encourage them to reject abortion as a solution to unplanned pregnancy.

It seems to me morally inconsistent and very unfair for a member of Congress to vote against abortion but then not support those economic measures, which experts say could cut abortions by as many as 500,000 in any given year.[5]

Kristin Day, who heads Democrats for Life (DFL), recently unveiled the organization's "95-10" Initiative, which is aimed at reducing abortions by 95 percent over the next 10 years.[6] In 2005, there were 1.3 million abortions in the United States.[7] A 95 percent reduction would cut that number to 65,000. Because this proposal does not advocate the criminalization of abortion, Day believes pro-choice Democrats may be willing to support the plan. The DFL plan does not include any provisions for contraceptives and contraceptive education, however, which is a drawback for many liberals in Congress, as well as for many Protestants, such as Eleanor Giddings Ivory of the Washington office of the Presbyterian Church (USA).[8] This omission is deemed significant among those who believe it is very important to give poor women access to contraception.

Support for the DFL proposals have coalesced around what is being called the Pregnant Women Support Act. This bill, sponsored by

Lincoln Davis, a Democratic member of Congress from Tennessee, has gained significant support from both sides of the political aisle, including Chris Smith, the Republican chair of the bipartisan Pro-Life Caucus in the House of Representatives, and Hillary Clinton in the Senate.[9]

I fully realize that a bill like the Pregnant Women Support Act is aimed primarily at lowering the number of abortions among poor women and in no way diminishes the inclination to have abortions among wealthier women, who often have abortions because a baby would disrupt their desired lifestyles. But the hard truth is that poor women are four times more likely to have unplanned pregnancies, five times more likely to have unintended births and three times more likely to have an abortion than their higher-income counterparts.[10] Money isn't everything, but it does impact the abortion rate in America.

For most Red Letter Christians, the issue comes down to whether or not a human fetus is a sacred human being created in God's image. If the answer to that question is yes, then abortion must be regarded as murder—and there is no doubt that murder is forbidden in Scripture. I find that many Red Letter Christians believe that something miraculous occurs at the moment of conception, that the zygote becomes much more than an assemblage of organic cells. Following in a tradition that goes all the way back to St. Augustine in the fourth century, it is at the moment when the egg is fertilized by a sperm that a living soul is created.

After that moment, that precious human being's life must be protected and cared for—both before and after his or her birth.

Other Points of View

Some Red Letter Christians are pro-life but nevertheless hold that abortions should be allowed in special cases, such as rape and incest. They also argue that there should be provisions to preserve the life of a pregnant woman via abortion if giving birth would cause her severe physical harm or even death. Trying to determine if giving birth poses such a threat would be difficult in many cases, and there is the rub. Such provisions in the law might easily be abused.

There are also several variants among pro-choice Red Letter Christians. For instance, some have a very hard time with late-term abortions. They hold to the belief that the embryonic child interacts with the mother during uterine development, and this interaction is the means by which the unborn is humanized (that is, becomes a sacred human being). The soul is not created through a biological process, they argue. Instead, it is through a spiritual, emotional and psychological interaction with the mother that the unborn grows into the image of God. That interaction, they say, begins eight or nine weeks after conception, at which time the fetus develops an operative brain and central nervous system capable of an interactive relationship with the mother. By the later stages of pregnancy, there is little question in their minds that this humanizing interaction is well under way and that aborting the unborn child is an act of murder.

Many pro-choice members of Congress agree with this interpretation of what makes a fetus human. Consequently, they voted in favor of the Partial-Birth Abortion Ban Act of 2003, while at the same time contending that they are pro-choice. They agree with the Roe v. Wade decision of the Supreme Court in 1973 that made room for abortions during the first trimester of pregnancy, but they are unable to support killing a human fetus after he or she has become viable.

To vote against abortion is, to some Red Letter Christians, a vote against the right of women to make decisions that determine their own biological destinies. They believe that whether or not a woman has an abortion should be a decision made by her and her doctor. Nobody, they say, other than the woman herself, should have control over what happens to her body. Many of these believers point to millennia of injustice against women, who for the better part of human history have had little control over how their bodies are used. They say that as Christians, we must do everything possible to end the oppression of women and empower them to make good and healthy choices for themselves.

The retort of pro-life advocates to this argument is that one person's freedom ends when it threatens the life of another. No one has the freedom to take someone else's life to serve his or her personal interests.

When It Comes to a Vote

When it comes to voting, both pro-life and pro-choice Red Letter Christians weigh their concerns on the abortion issue over and against such issues as their commitment to helping the poor, their opposition to war, their upset over what is happening to the environment, and their passion to see an end to racial prejudice and discrimination against the gay community. With such concerns looming large in their minds, pro-life Red Letter Christians might vote Democratic, in spite of the pro-choice plank in that party's platform.

Some pro-life Red Letter Christians often vote Democratic in spite of the party's official position. They make the case that abortions cannot significantly be curtailed by making them illegal. They are also convinced that those with enough money to circumvent the law would get abortions anyway, leaving those who can least afford it to either have unwanted babies or seek out dangerous means for aborting them. Furthermore, they suspect that making them illegal would only drive abortions underground. They have heard the stories about how abortions were performed before they were made legal: "back-alley abortions" by non-professionals, who sometimes sterilized or even killed women due to botched procedures or unsanitary conditions.

Regardless how we vote when considering the abortion issue, we will probably make some of our fellow Christians angry. This is not just another issue—for many, it is a life and death matter. But Red Letter

Christians must face the reality that there are good Christians on both sides of the debate. As hard as it may be, we must show grace toward those who take positions that differ from our own.

Contrary to what many think, the Bible does not speak specifically to the abortion issue. Pro-life advocates often quote Isaiah 49:1 to make their case, claiming that being "called" by God prior to birth supports their case that the unborn is a living soul. The verse reads:

> The LORD hath called me from the womb; from the bowels of my mother hath he made mention of my name (*KJV*).

On the other hand, those on the pro-choice side claim this very same verse to build their case. They argue that it is in the womb that the humanizing process that makes the unborn a sacred soul takes place—but only after the brain and nervous system become operative. This, they contend, allows for abortions during the earliest stage of pregnancy.

There is no easy way to decide the matter once and for all. Again, in the words of Scripture, you must "work out your own salvation with fear and trembling" (Phil. 2:12). Then carefully examine the positions of those running for office to determine how they have come to the positions they espouse and to see how their positions stand in relation to the one you believe is right.

CHAPTER 11

IMMIGRATION

There are heated and ongoing controversies about America's immigration policies. Not only are there serious questions about the future of U.S. immigration, there are also even more difficult questions concerning what to do about the more than 12 million undocumented immigrants already in our country, almost 60 percent of whom are estimated to have come from Mexico.[1] Considering how many there are, it seems unrealistic to hunt them down, arrest them and send them back from whence they came. Add to this difficulty the fact that many immigrant workers take jobs that most Americans do not want. For example, immigrants from south of the border are often glad to work certain industrial and farm jobs that are both arduous and low paying. It is safe to say that some of our country's economic enterprises, both industrial and agricultural, would shut down if it were not for illegal immigrants.

Besides the important work they do, there are other positive contributions made by both legal and illegal immigrants that we must consider. They pay taxes. In most cases, even illegal immigrants have taxes deducted from their salaries.[2] This is a fact often overlooked by critics who point out that social services such as schooling and medical help are regularly provided for immigrant families at the expense of taxpayers.

What is especially noteworthy is that many immigrants who have not been granted citizenship make regular payments into our nation's Social Security fund, yet are not entitled to the benefits of Social Security.[3] In addition, even legal immigrant workers with a Green Card are not likely to collect on the deductions paid to Social Security out of their salaries.[4] Questions should be raised by Red Letter Christians about whether or not there should be some corrective legislation to address the denial of Social Security benefits to legal workers. For now, however, older and disabled citizens who depend on Social Security ought to recognize that immigrants, both legal and illegal, are helping to keep America's Social Security fund solvent and monthly checks flowing their way.

High Walls, Wide Gates

As we consider the problem of illegal immigrants, we ought to be asking ourselves why these brothers and sisters do not try to enter our country legally. Entering illegally leaves them vulnerable to exploitation by unscrupulous employers who take advantage of their illegal status by underpaying them, and in the case of migrant agricultural workers, often providing them with substandard housing. There are far too many sweatshops, in places like New York City and Los Angeles, where workers endure extremely oppressive conditions because their employers threaten to expose them to authorities if they complain or try to quit. *So why don't they enter our country legally?*

Perhaps we might find the answer to that question if we take the time and the effort to examine what is required to be a legal immigrant and what is further required to become a U.S. citizen. It presently takes about three years and as much as $3,000 in legal fees to get the coveted Green Card required for legal residence and employment. In addition, each immigrant must have a U.S. citizen who will serve as a sponsor and be willing to assume any financial liabilities that the immigrant might incur.[5] Gaining citizenship status is even more difficult. In most cases it takes between 8 and 10 years and as much as $10,000 in legal fees.[6] Given these requirements, is it any wonder that the majority of the undocumented–who are overwhelmingly poor and looking for a better life for themselves and for their families–should cross our borders illegally?

On the other hand, we cannot ignore the justifiable arguments of the hardliners on immigration policy who rightly point out that, when people enter the United States illegally, we have no idea who is coming into our country and what dangers they may pose. How many of these illegal immigrants have criminal records? How many are drug smugglers? And in these troubling days, how many are would-be terrorists crossing our broken borders undetected?

Considering these differing points of view, I and other Red Letter Christians are in favor of establishing policies that erect "high walls" around our borders that have "wide gates." We should have high walls (figuratively speaking) in the form of strong border controls so that no one can enter our country without a background check and so that we can keep out foreign persons who pose a threat to our security and well-being. Our high walls, in turn, should have "wide gates" that welcome all those who hope to become a part of our community, with all the rights, privileges and responsibilities that entails. America's present greatness is built on the hardworking courage of generations of immigrant people who left their homes to seek a better life, and I believe our future greatness depends on how we welcome tomorrow's new Americans.

Recent attempts to pass corrective legislation on immigration have proved very controversial. One piece of legislation introduced to the Senate by Edward Kennedy (D-MA) and Jon Kyl (R-AZ) and all but killed in June 2007 would have allowed for the estimated 12 million illegal immigrants who arrived before January 1, 2007, to apply for legal resident status. In addition, these illegal immigrants could have become citizens if they wanted to do so, but (and this is a big *but*) there were very stringent requirements. The bill was 380 pages long and more complex than space allows for us to fully discuss here, but let's look at some broad outlines of what the bill proposed.

First, background checks would have to show that would-be legal immigrants who are in the country illegally have no criminal record. To both supporters and detractors of the bill, this is very reasonable. Second and third, however, illegal immigrants would have to return to their home countries within the next eight years to properly apply for re-entry, and would have to pay any back taxes they might owe in addition to a $5,000 fine per family. These last two requirements seem overly severe to more liberal critics of the legislation. When legal fees for citizenship are placed on top of these financial expectations, it's not likely that many will take advantage of the offer—especially because most of the immigrants in question lack the financial resources to comply.

In addition, the proposed bill would establish new criteria for determining who would be allowed back into the country, increasing the number of highly skilled workers, chosen on the basis of how they could serve our national interests. At the same time, the bill would reduce the total number of unskilled foreign workers legally admitted each year. Special exceptions would be made for farm workers.

If it were enforced, the section of the bill that could have the greatest effect on illegal immigration is the provision that would make it illegal for employers to hire anyone who cannot prove legal status as a "visiting" worker. Because the primary reason for sneaking into the United States is to get jobs, it is believed that this provision would do much to discourage illegal entrants.

It is easy to understand why liberals believed these conditions were too harsh on immigrants, and why they thought the conditions would add to the "brain drain" America is exercising on poorer nations of the world.

Conservatives also attacked the proposal, claiming that it was just another case of the failed amnesty policy put in place when Ronald

Reagan was president. Reagan offered legal status to illegal immigrants already in the country who were willing to register with the government, an offer that was to be followed up with strict controls on our borders. Conservative critics point out that this latter part of Reagan's policy was never carried out.

Conservatives also claimed (and many liberals agreed) that our borders are porous. There are few barriers and too few border guards. When violators of the law are caught crossing the borders illegally, the standard consequences involve little more than being packed up and sent home. Many of those who are returned to their countries of origin simply try illegal entry again–and eventually succeed. Critics of the bill wanted to know why it did not provide for fencing to be put up across our southern border, and why it did not give the police and courts means to deal more seriously with violators of the government's immigration laws.

On these critiques, many conservatives and liberals agree. When considering who you will choose to represent you, it's important to find out the pros and cons of upcoming legislation and the candidates' positions on the proposed laws so that you can make an informed and godly decision. This bill, which was endorsed by President Bush in spite of opposition from many conservatives in his own party, failed to pass. However, if Democrats gain additional seats in the Senate after the next election, it is likely that this same bill, with some modifications, will be reintroduced and made law.

The New Sanctuary Movement

Both the Hebrew Scriptures and the New Testament have much to say about immigrants. The Jews in ancient Israel were required to treat immigrants with kindness, respect and generosity, remembering that they too had once been aliens in a strange and distant land: "You shall not oppress a resident alien; you know the heart of an alien, for you were aliens in the land of Egypt" (Exod. 23:9).

Among the many things Jesus said about the treatment of outsiders or "strangers," perhaps the most familiar is in Matthew 25:31-46. This passage records Jesus telling His followers that they will be judged, both as a community and as individuals, on the basis of how welcoming they have been to the aliens at the gates.

Given what the Bible says, some church leaders—most often Roman Catholics—have decided to provide "sanctuary" for illegal immigrants sought by government authorities and ordered back to their countries of origin. Harking back to a medieval practice that kept civil authorities from arresting anyone inside a "sanctified" church building, these clergypersons are offering refuge to immigrants whom the courts have designated for deportation. They are especially likely to offer sanctuary when deportation would mean the separation of children from their parents. In the Southwest, there is at least one Roman Catholic bishop who has said that he is willing to go to jail rather than turn over to the police any immigrants who have sought sanctuary in the churches of his diocese.

What do you think about the practice of sanctuary? And what kind of answer will you look for when quizzing a candidate on this controversial matter?

Compassion and Justice

Most Christians agree that compassion and a commitment to biblical justice should motivate us when thinking through immigration policies, not only when considering those who want to come into our country to work, but also for those who want to come from nations where there is great oppression. Our laws *do* make provisions for political refugees to seek asylum in the United States, but they make little room for exceptions. And there are many cases where exceptions should be made. For instance, there are not sufficient provisions for refugees fleeing religious persecution. Consider Malaysia, where a woman who converts to Christianity without permission from her husband and the country's Islamic council can be jailed, and anyone trying to evangelize Muslims can be put to death. Are we willing to slam the door on those who seek a safe place to worship God freely?

Likewise, there is not enough leeway for those escaping socio-political oppression. Leading up to World War II, our government turned away thousands of Jews seeking escape from Nazi persecution because our immigration policies at the time had severe limits on certain European countries.[7] After many Hungarians fled their country following a revolt against the Soviet Union in the 1950s, they found that the "quota system" for immigration at the time would allow only a handful to enter the U.S., despite the fact that our government's *Voice of America* radio broadcasts had urged them to stage the revolt.[8] More recently, approximately 50,000 Iraqis a month flee their country because of the chaos created by our invasion. Because America does not presently define Iraq as a totalitarian state, Iraqi refugees have an extremely difficult time getting into our country. To date, less that 1,000 Iraqis have been admitted to the U.S. as refugees.[9] Compare that number to 30,000—the number of refugees from Iraq that have been welcomed to Sweden.[10] This comparison makes our country look miserly, considering that it was the U.S.-led invasion that created what is now a serious refugee problem.

When my father came to this country, he had no skills and no money, and he did not know the language. Nevertheless, this country made room for him. America gave him the chance to live out a dream for a better life for himself and his family. That kind of opportunity should still be available to people of goodwill who are willing to pledge allegiance to their new nation and live among us as people committed to the values and obligations that should be shared by all Americans.

Immigration legislation is a complicated matter, but whoever wants your vote at election time should have some ideas that will demonstrate biblically prescribed justice and compassion.

On the interior of the pedestal of the Statue of Liberty is a bronze plaque containing these words:

> Give me your tired, your poor,
> Your huddled masses yearning to breathe free,
> The wretched refuse of your teeming shore.
> Send these, the homeless, tempest-tost to me,
> I lift my lamp beside the golden door![11]

Candidates should be asked if Lady Liberty still extends this invitation on behalf of the American people.

CHAPTER 12

CRIME

According to the Justice Department's Bureau of Justice Statistics, U.S. prisons and jails added more than 42,000 inmates during the year ending June 30, 2006, the largest increase since 2000.[1] There are now 1.6 million people behind bars in America. When local jail populations are included, the total number of people jailed is about 2.2 million.[2] Six out of 10 of those incarcerated during that period of time were either black or Hispanic, and most had incomes below the poverty level.[3]

One out of every 30 men in our country commits a serious crime before the age of 40,[4] while only 12 percent of crimes committed result in convictions.[5] If these statistics are accurate, we must recognize that crime has become an epidemic in America, and that poverty and racism continue to heavily influence our justice system.

There have been many theories and explanations for this burgeoning crime rate in recent years. Democrats are likely to blame the Bush Administration for cutting monies out of the federal budget that, during the Clinton White House years, financed 50,000 additional police officers on the streets of U.S. cities.[6] Others believe that demographic factors are responsible. The cohort of men between the ages of 18 and 40 is much larger than it was a decade ago,[7] and because men in this age group are those most likely to commit crimes, it figures that an increase in crime over the past 10 years should have been expected.

Many preachers, backed up by the observations of social critics and pundits, claim that the increasing crime rate is the result of a collapsing social order. They point to a society that has lost its moral bearings and strayed from its religious foundations. There are accusations from pulpits that the values portrayed on television and in motion pictures, along with deviant messages in rock and rap music, have been major contributors to the disintegration of principles that make for a good and safe society. Much of what these preachers say is likely true.

Whatever the reason or reasons for the explosion of crime in America, we must take a hard look at possible solutions to determine how we can create a safer and saner nation for our children.

White-Collar Crime

Something that is often overlooked in the usual discussions about crime these days is the dramatic increase and influence of white-collar crime. I and many other sociologists believe that white-collar crimes exercise a huge power over a society's sense of well-being and may pose a greater threat than other kinds of crime. When government officials are exposed for having taken payoffs and when executives of major corporations are caught having deceived the public with inside stock trading, public trust is shaken. When leaders of industry are found to have concealed information about the dangers of products their companies put on the market, the public is hurt more, literally and psychologically, than by those whom we are more easily able to put behind bars.

Consider the millions of people who have died, along with the exorbitant costs to the public for health services, as a result of smoking. Yet the executives of cigarette companies had extensive knowledge of the health hazards of their products long before the Surgeon General of the United States made unequivocal announcements that cigarettes kill people.[8] Isn't such profit-seeking negligence criminal?

And what about the Enron scandal? Tens of thousands of men and women lost their jobs at Enron because of the "cooking of books," in which the company's top executives grossly overstated the corporations earnings, causing its collapse into bankruptcy. Thousands of others lost their life savings when the stock values of Enron disappeared.

In recent years, there has been disturbing news about the dealings of the Halliburton Corporation in Iraq. It's alleged that billions of dollars of taxpayer money cannot be accounted for. It has just disappeared.[9] Public confidence is undermined when records and minutes of meetings between Vice President Cheney and Halliburton executives are kept secret, while the vice president continues to collect back payment on bonuses from when he worked for that company.[10]

Or consider the impact of revelations about crooked political lobbyist Jack Abramoff, and the subsequent corruption investigation that has led to the convictions of two White House officials, a Congressman and nine other Washington insiders to date.[11] It's increasingly difficult for Americans to trust our political system when mounting evidence of its corruption is uncovered every day.

Add to these corporate and governmental crimes those committed by men and women in the field of medicine. There are more and more reports of deaths in hospitals that should be classified as manslaughter,[12] as well as an increase in the incidences of deception and overpricing of prescription medicines by pharmaceutical companies.[13] And when news of hospitals dumping homeless patients out on the street makes headlines, Americans begin to wonder if doctors still believe the part in the Hippocratic Oath in which they vow "to keep the good of the patient as the highest priority."[14]

White-collar criminals inspire cynicism among the public toward all who hold high office in business, health and government—even though the greater number of leaders in these arenas are trustworthy. The stability of a society is dependent on its citizens trusting its leaders, and white-collar criminality undermines that necessary trust.

The punishments for white-collar criminals are typically *very* lenient, especially when compared with penalties for so-called "blue-collar criminals." Sadly, church leaders and the heads of Christian charities have been reluctant to address white-collar crimes by calling for stricter sentences for those who perpetrate them. That may be because the people responsible for these sorts of crimes are often "upstanding" members of their congregations or church boards.

Recently I preached in a wealthy church in Durham, North Carolina. The pastor of this large and affluent congregation, knowing my feelings about the evils of the tobacco industry, was somewhat nervous about what I might say from the pulpit—he was afraid I would cause consternation among the executives and workers in his church who make their living in the "death" business. Believing I could not evade my responsibility to be forthright on the matter, he had cause for concern! When I got up to preach, I called into question how Christians could go on producing what they know is killing 450,000 Americans every year and causing incredible suffering for millions more. (It's easy to be prophetic and confrontational when you're catching a plane out of town in the afternoon. The pastor who stays to handle the fallout is the brave one.)

Red Letter Christians should be fearless in speaking the truth to industries that thrive by doing evil, and should pay special attention to where would-be lawmakers get the money to fund their campaigns. The tobacco and other industries make huge donations to the campaign chests of candidates on the state and national levels—such contributions have a way of protecting white-collar criminals when it's time for prosecution and sentencing.

Mandatory Sentencing

In recent years, there has been a tendency by those running for office who want to appear tough on crime to promise mandatory sentences for certain kinds of crime. This has resulted in many young people being put in jail for relatively minor offenses, such as being caught with marijuana cigarettes in their possession. Studies show that jailing young people is far more likely to inculcate criminal behavioral patterns than to discourage them,[15] so wouldn't it be best if the courts, with the help of social workers, decide sentences on a case-by-case basis? While they are still highly teachable and impressionable, don't we want to help our young people to make better decisions instead of consigning them to the company of older criminals who will teach them more effective ways to commit more crimes?

All mandatory sentencing should be questioned—the results of it are sometimes absurd. Consider the case of Weldon Angelos, a first-time offender who was sentenced in 2004 to 55 years for a small-time marijuana and gun conviction. The appeal for commutation of his sentence presently before President Bush was filed by the very judge who was forced by law to impose this extraordinarily stiff sentence.[16] So far, nothing has been done. Perhaps we can hope that the president will deem Weldon's mandatory sentence too harsh, just as he considered the 30-month sentence for lying before a federal grand jury passed on Scooter Libby, Vice President Cheney's former Chief of Staff, too harsh.

In another attempt to appear tough on crime, many states have enacted what are often called "three strikes and you're out" laws. These statutes propose that upon a third conviction, certain mandatory sentences be passed on offenders. This has also resulted in long imprisonments for relatively minor crimes. Such "three strikes" laws prevent judges and juries from passing sentences that best serve the interests of both society and those convicted. Voters must think about whether such laws are just and reasonable. If the conclusion is that they are not, inquiries should be made about what candidates running for office will pledge to do about repealing them.

Capital Punishment

There is another topic related to the issue of crime that must be taken on by Red Letter Christians: capital punishment. When Saddam Hussein was hung, British Prime Minister Tony Blair declared in no uncertain terms that he was personally opposed to capital punishment on moral grounds.[17] He opposed the execution of Saddam Hussein in spite of the horrendous crimes against humanity Hussein had committed. I wish our own president held to the same conviction. Both Tony Blair and George Bush are professing Christians, and that they differ so greatly when it comes to capital punishment is evidence of how two people who seem equally sincere in their convictions can have diametrically opposing points of view.

I will abandon any attempt to set forth two sides and say boldly and unequivocally that capital punishment should not be supported by those who claim to be followers of Christ. Contrary to the opinions of some who think otherwise, I believe the red letters of the Bible disallow capital punishment, regardless of the crime.

My reasons for opposing capital punishment arise from Matthew 5:7, where we read that Jesus said, "Blessed are the merciful, for they shall receive mercy." It seems clear to me that, according to Jesus' Sermon on the Mount, mercy is required of Christians even when dealing with capital crimes.

There are those who will argue that the Bible prescribes an eye for an eye, a tooth for a tooth, a life for a life (see Exod. 21:24; Lev. 24:20; Deut. 19:21). They say this means that the punishment should equal the crime—a person found guilty of killing another person should be put to death. To that, I respond by pointing out that Jesus proposed that we transcend the principle of retributive justice by giving us a new commandment. I don't think it's presumptuous to claim that when Jesus gives a *new* commandment, He wills that the new commandment supersede the old.

The apostle Paul picked up the theme begun by Jesus when he wrote that we should "overcome evil with good" (Rom. 12:21). How can we honestly suggest that killing a person made in God's image does so, regardless of their trespasses?

While capital punishment is widely accepted among Evangelicals, Red Letter Christians largely oppose it. In this respect, Red Letter Christians are more in harmony with their Roman Catholic and mainline Protestant brothers and sisters, whose churches' teachings forbid capital punishment.

As we seek solutions to the problems caused by crime, there are a seemingly limitless number of proposals deserving of consideration. I'd like to call your attention to one proposal in particular, a bill presented to Congress that would offer probation to incarcerated prisoners who are first-time offenders more than 45 years of age whose crimes were of a non-violent nature.[18] Such prisoners, if released, would not likely be dangerous to the general public, and if they were properly supervised and their activities carefully circumscribed, their release could save taxpayers a great deal of money. (It costs nearly $40,000 per year to keep a prisoner incarcerated.[19]) The bill also has requirements for those released to be involved in community service programs. Advocates of this legislation say these components together would be a step toward reforming and improving our approach to crime. Sadly, the bill has been tabled by Congress and is not likely to be considered for a vote in the near future.

Candidates should be asked if they would support such a bill and, if elected, work to get it on the floor for a vote. Shouldn't jail cells be reserved primarily for violent criminals? Why keep so many elderly non-violent criminals behind bars while those who pose a serious threat to society walk among us because there is no space for them in our overcrowded prisons?

Principles to Guide Us

When contemplating how we should deal with criminals, we must look within Scripture to discern principles that can guide us.

In the ancient world, response to crime was almost always retributive, but a careful review of biblical teachings shows us that God calls us to answers other than retribution. Here are four responses to criminals that I believe emerge out of a careful reading of Scripture:

1. Repentance
2. Restitution
3. Reconciliation
4. Restoration

When evil is done, the first thing that should be asked of the perpetrator is *repentance*. In our present judicial system, this is usually not the case.

Sometimes criminals are not aware of the significance of the harm they have done to their victims, and so little in the way of repentance is forthcoming. For instance, studies done by criminologists give evidence that many rapists are able to convince themselves that their victims actually "enjoyed" what happened to them and only reported it as a crime to protect their reputations.[20]

One proposal that I believe should become part of the sentencing process would give victims of crimes the opportunity to tell offenders about the damage that was inflicted by their criminal acts. Victims would be given the chance to confront their offenders in the courtroom, either face to face or by video.

Rapists need to hear from victims who have debilitating nightmares and live in constant fear. They need to hear firsthand about the mental and emotional anguish their victims suffer from such violation. They need to know how the rape has damaged the victims' relationships with others, in some cases leading to divorce.

Often thieves are prone to minimize the damage they did to their victims by telling themselves that insurance companies will cover the losses of those from whom they stole. Those who have been robbed should have the opportunity to explain how they feel anxious and afraid because a stranger has probed and handled their personal belongings. Thieves need to hear how the victims have lost any sense of security in their own homes. Such confrontations and explanations could bring the offenders to repentance.

Too often what is presented as repentance is simply regret over being caught. A person might say "I'm sorry" but be sorry only about impending punishment. True repentance is when an offender is overcome with remorse over the loss and suffering an innocent victim has had to endure because of the wrong he or she has done.

Biblically, repentance is the first thing required of the sinner. We need to look for candidates who understand this, who do not see an emphasis on repentance as a sign of being "soft on crime."

Restitution is the second consideration that deserves our attention as we think about what we can do to help transform criminals into good and decent citizens. In Luke 19:1-10, we read about Zacchaeus, a tax collector who was a "sellout" to the Roman conquerors of Israel. He had become rich, exploiting the position of power given to him by defrauding his fellow Jews.

We find in his encounter with Jesus an excellent example of how someone can make restitution to those whom they have wronged. His acceptance by Jesus in spite of his despicable behavior drove Zacchaeus to make reparations to all who had been the victims of his crooked dealings. He promised Jesus that he would return fourfold whatever he had stolen.

At first, this seemingly overgenerous offer appears merely as an exuberant expression of gratitude in response to Jesus' grace, going beyond what we would have expected. That is, until we learn that returning fourfold is exactly what God's law, as found in Exodus 22:1, requires to make reparations for stealing. Exodus 21 and 22 give a long list of requirements for the restitution required for various crimes. The Bible teaches that those who have done wrong and want to make things right must compensate those they have harmed, and restitution should be part of our approach to criminals today.

Restitution can help repentant criminals by providing some alleviation of guilt and anxiety, and it can also diminish the sense of loss experienced by the victims. After a criminal is released from prison, that person is said to have "paid his or her debt to society." *But it wasn't society that was robbed!* cries the victim. *It was me! And nobody has paid me back for my loss!*

In a case I learned about from Daniel VanHess, a worker with Chuck Colson's Prison Fellowship, an 18-year-old offender had been caught after having broken into several houses in his neighborhood to steal more than $15,000 worth of goods. At his trial, rather than sending the thief to jail, the judge handed down a very creative sentence. First, he had the young man do community service every Saturday—cleaning up the neighborhood, painting homes and fixing up the playground. Second, he was required to pay restitution to the victims. He had to pay back what the stolen goods were worth, which was far more than he had been paid when he fenced the items. Third, he was required to sell everything he owned, including his car, and put the money from these sales into the restitution fund. Finally, he had to sit down and face the angry people who had been robbed and hear what they had to say. Amazingly, through repentance and restitution, the young man and his victims were reconciled, eventually becoming friends.

We should continue to seek creative solutions to criminal behavior like this one. It seems to me that we should look for candidates who understand the importance of restitution both for the victim and for the offender, and who are willing to consider ways in which restitution can be made—perhaps even after jail time has been served.

Next, we must give careful consideration to *reconciliation*. In God's dealings with us, the goal has always been to bring about reconciliation. Jesus was sent into the world so that through Him we might be reconciled to God. We, having been reconciled, are called in turn to carry out a ministry of reconciliation with others (see 2 Cor. 5:18-19).

When a crime has been committed, we must attempt to bring about reconciliation between the offender and the victim. Obviously, there are circumstances and situations that make this appear impossible—but with God, all things are possible.

During the revolution in Nicaragua in the 1970s, a Sandinista commander in the revolutionary army named Tomás Borge was taken prisoner by the military loyal to the dictator, Anastasio Samoza. While in prison, Borge was castrated; then, while he was chained to the wall of his cell, they brought in his wife and gang raped her. We can only imagine the intensity of hatred that Borge must have felt toward those horrible men.

When the revolution ended with the triumph of the revolutionary Sandinistas, Tomás Borge was taken from the prison and marched in a triumphal parade down the main street of Managua. The people of the capital city lined the sidewalks and cheered as the heroes of the revolution marched by. As Borge waved at the cheering crowds, he spotted a face he could never forget, the face of one of the soldiers who had participated the day he was castrated and his wife was raped before his eyes. Leaving the parade, Borge rushed over to the man, grabbed him by the shoulders and shook him, shouting, "Do you recognize me? Do you know who I am? Is my face familiar to you?"

The terrified man tried to pretend he didn't know Tomás Borge, but Borge wouldn't let up. He repeated, over and over again, "I know who you are! I will never forget you! Never! Never! Never!"

Then Borge yelled, "Do you understand why we had this revolution? Do you understand what this revolution was all about? Do you understand now?"

Shaken and trembling, the stunned man answered, "Yes! Yes! I understand! I understand!"

"No, you don't!" responded Tomás Borge. With that, he embraced the man and shouted, "*This* is what the revolution was about—I forgive you! This is what the revolution is all about."[21]

By the grace of God, seemingly impossible reconciliations are possible.

Finally, the goal in dealing with criminals must be *restoration*. There must be attempts to restore the offender to what God intended for him or her. In this task, the Church can do much. For example, when the goal is to reunite the offender with his or her family upon being released from prison, finding the family a place to live and a decent paying job is part of the restoration process, and the Church can help. Restoration gives back to the offender not only life as it was before the crime, but also the life God meant for him or her to have. We must remember these words of Scripture:

> My friends, if anyone is detected in a transgression, you who have received the Spirit should restore such a one in a spirit of gentleness. Take care that you yourselves are not tempted (Gal. 6:1).

A major problem in helping those released from prison gain restoration is that they carry criminal records with them for the rest of their lives. This can become a major barrier to employment and sometimes even in their opportunity to live in certain neighborhoods.

Ron Acton, the executive director of the Cabrini Green Legal Aid Clinic (CGLA) in Chicago, has struggled with this problem in his ministry. His faith-based organization is deeply committed to facilitating the re-entry of ex-felons back into society. Acton explains that presently the only real way to clear the record of a felon's past crimes is for the president, or in some cases, the governor of a state, to grant a pardon.

Acton's suggestion is to change constitutional law so that certain judges would also have the right to grant pardons in particular cases. Obviously, it would be essential that the criminal records of some felons be kept available, particularly in cases wherein violent and sexual crimes have been committed. However, there are some cases wherein sustaining criminal records is unjust.

As a case in point, Acton cites a situation in which a Hispanic woman who was wrongly accused of a drug charge was urged by her public defender to plead guilty and receive a suspended sentence, resulting in a felony on her record. The woman, who spoke almost no English, did not understand the consequences of pleading guilty and only later discovered that her criminal record would keep her from getting a job. The governor was asked by the lawyers at the CGLA to grant her a pardon. But the governor, in a hurried decision, rejected her appeal. According to Ron Acton, this is a case in which careful consideration by a fair-minded judge would have aided the restoration of this woman and corrected a shortcoming of the criminal justice system.

But because it is improbable that there will be constitutional changes that permit judges to grant such pardons, Acton says the next best thing would be to allow the records of felons, in specially determined cases, to be sealed and only made available through due process of law. He believes this provision should be made available to felons who have a record of good behavior for an extended period of time (e.g., 20 years) following the completion of their sentences.

At the very least, Acton argues, arrangements must be made so that those who have made significant progress in rehabilitation and have no new blemishes on their records might have notes and explanations attached to their records so that potential employers or landlords would know about their successful efforts toward good citizenship.

How to deal with the records of felons and other matters surrounding restoration of criminals should be considered by candidates up for election, and it is up to Red Letter Christians to bring these matters to their attention. If we are to fulfill the biblical obligation to care for those in prison (see Matt. 25:31-46), we cannot turn away from standing up for ex-felons as they try to make their way back into everyday life. We must be a voice for those who have no voice.

There are some things the law can do, but there are others that can only come by the grace of God, as that grace is expressed through the Church. Every church—and I do mean *every* church—should have a prison ministry. Part of that ministry should be to visit those who are incarcerated. Another part should be to minister to the families of those in prison, and especially to provide loving help for the children of those prisoners. Most important, the Church should be a welcoming fellowship that gives to those who have been released from prison a caring community that will help them in all ways possible into full restoration. Jesus has called the Church to such a ministry.

THE ECONOMIC ISSUES

SECTION FOUR

CHAPTER 13

THE FEDERAL BUDGET

Budgets are moral documents. Jesus said that where your treasure is, there your heart will be also (see Matt. 6:21). This truth applies to individuals, families, churches and certainly to governments.

Politically, budgets reflect the values and priorities of a township, city, state or nation. They tell us what is most important to the elected officials who make up the budgets, and by extension, what is most important to those they represent. Examining these priorities is an obligation for those of us who call ourselves Red Letter Christians.

When all is said and done, most of what elected officials do is to decide what to do with our tax dollars. Whether the war in Iraq ends or continues will be determined by whether or not Congress and the president choose to fund it. What happens with regard to Social Security, Medicare, Medicaid and other entitlement programs will depend on the political commitments of those we send to Washington to represent our interests. The values espoused by those we put in the White House or elect to Congress will determine how many of our tax dollars will be spent to subsidize farmers to grow grain sold on foreign markets and how much will be spent on daycare for children of low-income working parents. How much money will be spent funding the Palestinian Authority or the State of Israel, how much will be spent to help eliminate hunger in developing nations, how much will be spent to underwrite the auto and oil industries—all will be decided when the vote is taken on the federal budget.

I think it's fair to say that, more than anything else, our votes influence how the government spends our money.

Politicians know that they can't finance every good thing that could or should be done. Most of them will tell you that they favor causes such as saving the environment, addressing the AIDS crisis in Africa, improving education for socially disinherited children, making our ports secure against terrorists, and putting more police on the streets of dangerous neighborhoods. But how much money they are willing to budget for any one of these concerns is highly influenced by what they believe matters most to voters back home in their districts—after all, they are elected to represent those voters! In many cases, however, politicians' budgeting priorities are also determined by the concerns of special-interest groups that have helped to finance their campaigns.

The (Im)Morality of the Budget

As I try to provide an overview of the federal budget and what many Red Letter Christians are saying about it, the facts and figures may set your head spinning. The terminology and the details provided by the government are almost beyond comprehension for most of us. But stick with me—if budgets are moral documents, we need to be aware of the values that they represent.

It is easy to find people on both sides of the political aisle ready to denounce the federal budgets that have been proposed over the last several years. Such denunciations are usually based on who is helped and who is hurt by what is and is not appropriated in those budgets. The 2007 budget, for example, caused consternation among many Christians for a variety of reasons.

First, there was concern that the 2007 budget gave huge benefits to rich people—who do not need and often have not even asked for them—without doing much for poor people. If priorities are not changed, those with annual incomes of more than a million dollars will receive tax cuts averaging $162,000 a year by the year 2012, when the tax laws made during the Bush Administration will have taken full effect.[1] Studies by the Brookings Institute show that by 2012, those households that have incomes that put them in the top 1 percent of the population (more than $400,000 a year) will receive $67,000 a year in tax breaks.[2] On the other hand, Americans with low or middle incomes will receive relatively little in the way of benefits, and will possibly lose many of the benefits they presently enjoy.[3]

Second, some "entitlement programs"—that is, programs that guarantee benefits by agreement of law—had to be eliminated or significantly cut back in order to compensate for the loss of tax revenues under the 2007 budget. There were planned cuts of up to $283 billion in domestic programs. These included:

- The elimination of the Commodity Supplemental Food Program, which costs about $20 per month for each of 440,000 needy elderly Americans for the purchase of food

- Cutting $420 million from the Low-Income Home Energy Assistance Program, which helps millions of poor, elderly and disabled Americans afford to heat their homes during the winter

- Cutting the Head Start Program by $100 million. Because teachers' salaries (along with other expenses) rise with inflation, Head Start programs will either have to reduce the number of children served or reduce the number of teachers available to serve them.

- Cutting funding for public housing to 5.9 percent below its 2006 level, and cutting Supportive Housing for the Elderly and People with Disabilities to 28 percent below its 2006 level

- Cutting funding for elementary and secondary education by $6.9 billion over the next five years

- Cutting funding for pollution control and abatement by $1.4 billion[4]

The list goes on and on.

There were some who cheered these cuts, claiming that waste and fiscal mismanagement in federally funded entitlement programs were responsible for the high costs of these services. They asserted that cuts in funding were needed to force more responsible spending and to enable the government to serve needy people more effectively.

Conservatives rightly point out that increased spending does not necessarily mean increased benefits. A good example to make their case can be found in spending for education.

In Camden, New Jersey, a city to which I alluded earlier as having a high school dropout rate of more than 50 percent, the superintendent of schools was given an annual salary of $220,000 and a discretionary budget of $400 a month for "gas allowance."[5] Compare that amount with the district's appropriation of just $18,000 per year to educate each child.[6]

Obviously, the failures of the Camden school system are not wholly the result of a lack of dollars. Other major problems are responsible for the failures of this school system, including wasted spending on a bloated administrative staff and corrupt fiscal practices. Add to this the difficulty of educating children from dysfunctional homes (which in Camden is more the norm than the exception) and the facts that the typical child in Camden watches television six hours a day,[7] that drugs permeate right down to the elementary level and that the physical dangers posed for both teachers and pupils drive the best of them to leave public schools to teach and learn in more secure environments.

I am in no way suggesting through this example that we shouldn't put more money toward paying our educators higher salaries, or that we shouldn't spend on programs that benefit at-risk children. If we want to attract the brightest and best into the incredibly important and difficult vocation of teaching, we must improve financial incentives for them, and we all know that spending on Head Start programs, special after-school tutoring and lunch programs for poor children have positive effects. But money, as important as it is, will not solve many of the major problems faced by some school districts. More money for failing schools is not always the answer.

Endangered Entitlements

Stories like that of the Camden school district cause many fiscal conservatives to throw up their hands and call for drastic cuts in all entitlement programs. An article in the *Wall Street Journal* in January 2007 named "entitlements" as the primary cause of a possible fiscal collapse of the federal government by the year 2050.[8] The article declared that these programs must be cut for the nation to survive.

Increased costs of Medicare and Medicaid are growing at a much faster rate than is the economy, driven by the dramatic rise in annual costs for each person served by America's healthcare system.[9] New technologies are improving healthcare in dramatic ways, and these new technologies are expensive. It is inconceivable that all Americans will not want to avail themselves of all the new scientific developments in medical care, and the budgetary consequences are all too obvious.

Given these rising healthcare costs, it is surprising that the Bush Administration proposed cuts in Medicaid funding in future budgets. The president proposed a total of $24.7 billion over five years and $60.9 billion over 10 years for Medicaid—these vast amounts are actually *reductions* in federal spending.[10] His administration asked that these reductions be compensated by shifting some of the costs of Medicaid from the federal government to the states. Under this proposal, for example, the federal government and state governments would share the costs of such things as inspecting nursing homes for quality and safety. Some of this is already being done, but in the future the share shouldered by the states would be increased significantly: Almost $21 billion of the annual costs of Medicaid would be shifted from the federal level to state budgets.[11] Faced with this heavy extra financial burden, states would have to choose between cutting back on their Medicaid programs by reducing eligibility, benefits and payments to providers of healthcare, or cutting back on other state-sponsored programs.

The net results of these proposed federal budget initiatives would likely mean the poor losing out on healthcare. The Bible teaches that "religion that is pure and undefiled before God, the Father, is this: to care for orphans and widows in their distress, and to keep oneself unstained by the world" (Jas. 1:27). Given that teaching, Christians cannot allow the neglect of financially distressed widows and orphans who need medical care.

I believe, unfortunately, that churches are unlikely to step forward to compensate poor people for what they will lose in terms of government-funded healthcare, despite the declarations of politically conservative Evangelicals who contend that the Bible tells churches to do so rather than ask the government to help. On call-in Christian talk radio shows across the nation, it is common to hear the hosts, as well as those who call in, complain that the government is stealing from people when it takes money (by way of tax dollars) from those who have it and uses it to help the poor. Charity, they say, should be a *voluntary* activity, done out of the goodness of our hearts. Citing Galatians 6:2-10, they argue that helping the poor is a task God has given to Christians, which should be carried by the Church.

Whether or not you agree with those who make this claim, you must ask yourself honestly if America's churches are ready to assume this task. And if churches are not ready to meet the needs of the poor, then ought we not turn to the government, managing our tax dollars, to care for them?

Red Letter Christians have no problem viewing the government as a possible instrument of God. We believe that Christ is at work outside the Church as well as in it, and that we are called to participate with those in the world through whom God's will is being done. We are ready to join with people of goodwill outside the Church who work through the government and by other means to help the poor. When we do so, we believe we are joining Christ where He is bringing His Kingdom to earth, a Kingdom where "the blind receive their sight, the lame walk, the lepers are cleansed, the deaf hear, the dead are raised, and the poor have good news brought to them" (Matt. 11:5).

There are many people who do not claim Jesus as Lord who nevertheless endeavor to work for what they call the "common good." We read about people like this in Romans 2:13-15:

> For it is not the hearers of the law who are righteous in God's sight, but the doers of the law who will be justified. When Gentiles, who do not possess the law, do instinctively what the law requires, these, though not having the law, are a law to themselves. They show that what the law requires is written on their hearts, to which their own conscience also bears witness.

Reading this passage of Scripture, we Red Letter Christians are convinced that working for the "common good" with both those inside and outside the Christian community can solve the problems surrounding Medicare, Medicaid, Social Security and public assistance for poor children. And we have no problem with tax dollars from all Americans being used to such Kingdom ends.

The Special Case of Social Security

Everyone realizes that Social Security is a budget expense headed off the charts. The annual report on the financial status of the Social Security Trust Fund released in April 2007 showed that we will face a serious crisis when "baby boomers" (those born immediately following World War II) become eligible to receive retirement benefits. The report showed that reserves in the fund will be exhausted by 2041.[12] This doesn't mean payment of benefits will be cut off at that time, but that Social Security will be able to pay only 75 percent of scheduled benefits instead of the full amounts promised.

Without going into the minute details, it's projected that by 2017, benefit payments will begin to exceed the amount of money Social Security takes in through payroll taxes.[13] At that point, in order to keep paying benefits, it will become necessary for the agency to start redeeming the bonds it presently holds, which were established for the investment of its reserves. By 2041, however, there will be no more bonds left to redeem. From then on, unless something changes, payment of benefits will have to be made directly from funds that come in from payroll taxes. And taxes will be able to finance only 75 percent of promised benefits.

While there are no immediate problems with making Social Security payments, concern about the long-term shortfall that will begin in 2017 should lead us to reconsider the impact of extending the 2001 and 2003 tax cuts instituted by the Bush Administration. Eliminating those tax cuts would, according to the Center on Budget and Policy Priorities, mean that the federal government would take in three times as much money over the next 75 years as it would have to pay out for increases in Social Security over the same period of time.[14] On the other hand, making the tax cuts permanent means the federal government will *lose* three times as much money over the next 75 years as it will cost for increases in Social Security.[15]

The question should be raised with candidates about an end to the Bush tax cut program, with money from the possible increase in tax revenue going into Social Security. It seems to me that this is one possible way to save the Social Security system in the short run, and may even be a long-term solution.

A special commission was put together in 1983 that studied problems related to the long-term financing of Social Security, and then made recommendations to then-President Ronald Reagan.[16] In response, he initiated a variety of modest benefit reductions and revenue-raising measures, and the system was strengthened. It took courage on Reagan's part to act on the commission's recommendations because he upset a lot of elderly folks. Similar courage is needed today, but to date, few have shown themselves up to the challenge. The idea of cutting back payment of benefits undoubtedly will encounter great opposition in Congress, regardless of which party is in power, but we should look for candidates who are willing to bite the bullet and do what needs to be done.

In 2005, President Bush tried to initiate a plan to address the situation, but Congress refused to pass it into law.[17] It involved, among other proposals, that a certain amount of what individuals annually pay into Social Security be set aside and made available to taxpayers to decide for themselves how their money should be invested. His idea was that, through investments, a higher income could be possible for individual Americans, and that wise investments might compensate for losses when cuts become necessary after 2041. But Bush's plan came under immediate fire from those who claimed that, while the plan might provide a financial bonanza for Wall Street brokers, it might just as well lead those with no knowledge about investing into losing much of what otherwise would have been guaranteed retirement income.

If you're confused, join the club! I've thought long and hard about this issue, trying to figure out a foolproof way to make the Social Security system work into the indefinite future, and I must admit that I'm perplexed. Two things I do know: First, to lay all blame for ballooning federal deficits at the door of maintaining Social Security is not fair or accurate. I and others strongly believe that Bush's tax policies, along with the costs of the war in Iraq, are the main reasons for our nation's growing deficits. Second, even if candidates do not have answers to the problems posed by the present Social Security system, we should expect them to be aware of the facts and figures related to the problems and to be fearless in proposing difficult solutions.

Caring for the elderly is very much a biblically prescribed obligation. The prophets declared that the kind of society God will bless is one in which elderly people live out the fullness of their lives in health and well-being (see Isa. 65:20). When we read in the Ten Commandments that we are to honor our mothers and fathers, we should realize this means that we are to care for them in their old age (see Exod. 20:12).

And caring for the elderly who do not have financial means to care for themselves is not only a *family* obligation. Red Letter Christians will not leave to suffer those whose children are unwilling or who do not have the means to care for them. We all know that people are living longer than ever before. We also know that the cost of caring for the elderly is skyrocketing. This makes it impossible for many children, individually, to fulfill the obligation of providing for their parents.

What makes matters worse is that our consumer lifestyles keep most people from saving and investing money for what have been called their "golden years." Sermonizing about all that is wrong with being caught up in America's present consumer-craze doesn't seem to do much good these days. But when we look at the various problems that come with caring for the elderly, we realize the urgency of saving the Social Security system. Without it, the future may present us with some horrible scenarios.

The Budget's Future

There is no telling what the federal budget will look like in the years to come. As of this writing, the Senate Budget Committee has adopted a resolution to provide increased defense spending in accord with President Bush's requests for the years 2008 through 2012.[18] On top of the defense appropriations for these fiscal years, a total of $285 billion in "emergency" funding for the war in Iraq has been approved for the years 2007, 2008 and 2009.[19] Even *without* the emergency funding for the war, the president's defense budget for 2008 represents an 8.5 percent increase over what was appropriated for 2007 (adjusted for inflation).[20]

On the other hand, a relatively small increase was budgeted for non-defense discretionary programs in 2008: just $6 billion more than in the 2007 budget.[21] Such non-defense items include programs in education, transportation and environmental protection. In an effort to reduce the government's deficit spending, the president had actually requested a $10 billion *cut* in non-defense programs[22]—so this increase was not especially welcomed by those in his administration.

Do not be seduced by the argument that we must spend heavily on the military if we are to keep up with China and Russia in the arms race, even in light of the fact that President Vladimir Putin has vowed to strengthen the Russian military. That argument is downright silly when you consider that in 2007, the U.S. spent $528.7 billion on its military, while China spent $49.5 billion and Russia spent $34.7 billion.[23] *Our military spending was 11 times that of China's and almost 16 times that of Russia's.* In 2008, our military spending is projected to be over $560 billion.[24]

The prophet Isaiah warned the ancient Jews not to trust in military might for their security. He said:

> Alas for those who go down to Egypt for help and who rely on horses, who trust in chariots because they are many and in horsemen because they are very strong, but do not look to the Holy One of Israel or consult the LORD! (Isa. 31:1).

If Isaiah were with us today, what do you think he might say about America's federal budget? Might he tell us that the strength of a nation does not depend on our armies, but on living out what has been called "the Micah challenge"?

> He has told you, O mortal, what is good; and what does the LORD require of you but to do justice, and to love kindness, and to walk humbly with your God? (Mic. 6:8).

Some Christians believe that living out love and justice for poor and oppressed people is a good thing, but they do not believe it to be a substitute for military might when dealing with the rest of the world. We who are Red Letter Christians think otherwise and argue that there will be more security for our nation if we change our budget priorities and use our enormous national resources to care for the poor who need our help. We know that there are evil people in the world, but we also know that it is possible to overcome evil with good (see Rom. 12:21).

Sound like foolishness? Well, who ever said that living out the lifestyle prescribed by Jesus was anything else?

CHAPTER 14

THE MINIMUM WAGE

The federal minimum wage is too low. If the average American is to earn enough money to pay rent, buy food and care for the other necessities of life, the minimum wage needs to be raised to at least $9.00 an hour. This is the amount needed to take care of *one person*. There's no way a worker can support a spouse—let alone care for children—with such a low income.

Any improvement for those who have a hard time making ends meet deserves our applause, so I hesitantly cheer a recent act of Congress that raised the minimum wage from $5.15 to $5.85 an hour. But although it will further increase to $7.25 by the summer of 2009, this addresses the problem only in a very limited way.

Consider the fact that the minimum wage had not been raised for almost a decade, and that during that time, the inflation rate climbed annually at a rate of around 6 percent. It doesn't take a mathematical genius to figure out that the recent increase of the minimum wage doesn't nearly compensate for the decline in buying power due to inflation. In fact, 80 percent of Americans have lost $2,300 in buying power (given the present value of the dollar) over the last eight years.[1]

And consider that in many parts of the country, the cost of real estate has climbed dramatically, greatly outdistancing the earnings of typical employees. This means that buying a house can no longer be part of the American dream for a significant part of the American workforce.

For and Against a Wage Increase

In recent months I have been on a variety of Christian radio shows, expressing my concerns about the declining economic power of those who work at or near the minimum wage. In every case, when I made the proposal to raise the minimum wage, the responses from both interviewers and listeners were swift and usually angry.

"Don't you realize that we'd be driving up wages and that this would lead to many small companies being driven out of business?" was one common response.

If taking this step would pose a threat to entrepreneurs, there is much the federal government could do to ease the strain. My friend and one-time head of the government's Small Business Administration, Phil Lader, says that simply cutting the amount of paperwork small-business owners have to deal with would decrease their costs of operations significantly. In many instances, small companies have to fill out the same number of forms and meet the same reporting requirements as big companies like General Motors and IBM. The costs for such paperwork is the same for a small business as it is for a big one, but these costs eat up a much greater part of a small business's profits. There is much the government could do to help small businesses overcome this inequity and become more profitable and easily able to pay livable wages.

One angry radio talk show host asked, "Do you realize that raising the minimum wage will make it less likely for employers to hire teens and college students for summer jobs? Is that what you want? And what do you think those teenagers will do when they are left to fend for themselves on city streets with nothing to keep them occupied? And what will you offer to all those college students who won't be able to find summer jobs or earn the money they need to return to school in the fall?"

To those who say that raising the minimum wage would keep employers from hiring teenagers for summer jobs, I offer the suggestion that exceptions to the higher wage be made for workers 16 years of age and younger.

The most common comeback to my proposal was that raising the minimum wage would drive employers to move their companies and industries out of the country to places like India and China, where labor costs are cheaper. A mandatory increase in wages, it was said, would lead to the exporting of jobs to other countries and result in hundreds of thousands of Americans losing their employment.

In response to these fears, I suggest that serious consideration be given to a proposal offered by former Vice President Gore during his presidential campaign in 2000. Gore proposed that, through the World Trade Organization and the United Nations, a minimum wage be established for all workers who produce goods and services that involve international transactions. It would not have to be high—perhaps as low as $2.50 an hour. Even at that level, such a minimum wage would not only go a long way toward ending exploitation of women and children in Third World sweatshops, it would also make American employers more likely to keep their business right here in the United States.

Shipping business and industry overseas is not the gigantic bargain that it seems at first. The costs of dealing with language and cross-cultural misunderstandings can be enormous. Then there's the cost of shipping manufactured goods long distances. Add to those the cost of trade tariffs and the illegal payoff of foreign customs officials (yes, such payments are common), and the bargains in labor costs begin to disappear. If we could factor in the increased costs of production and services overseas and invest the difference into paying fair wages at home, the advantages for companies exporting jobs could disappear completely.

Some may react by crying out that implementing Al Gore's proposal would raise the cost of what we now purchase at bargain prices at places like Wal-Mart. *Exactly!* But isn't it time for Christians to admit that we should reject bargains if they are gained by the exploitation of the poorest of the poor in developing countries? Isn't it time for Red Letter Christians to state loud and clear that we are willing to buy less in order that justice for oppressed workers can become increasingly possible?

Over all these arguments against raising the minimum wage was the image imprinted on my mind of "the Burger King mom," so vividly described by my friend Jim Wallis, founder and editor of *Sojourners* magazine. Jim once told of being in a Burger King in Washington, DC, and noticing that the woman waiting on customers at the counter would, from time to time, hurry from behind the register to check out what was going on at a table in the corner. Seated there were two little boys doing their homework.

Jim immediately sized up the situation: This was a working mom, keeping her eyes on her children to see that they stayed out of trouble while at the same time trying to earn enough money to keep her bills paid. She was a struggling member of that group of Americans often referred to as "the working poor." It's likely that this diligent mother was also one of the 47 million Americans with no medical coverage for herself or her children[2]—and daycare was obviously not an option, or her boys would have been there.

For just a moment, imagine what life must be like for her and her little family, trying to live on her minimum wage.

Shouldn't there be a better deal for a woman like this? Shouldn't Christians be concerned? Shouldn't Red Letter Christians join with those who plead with Congress to raise the minimum wage?

God-driven or Market-driven Wages?

When considering this issue, we have to ask what the Bible says. While the words that speak to this most directly are not in red letters, we must pay serious attention to what is written in Scripture. In the book of James, we read:

> Come now, you rich people, weep and wail for the miseries that are coming to you. Your riches have rotted, and your clothes are

> moth-eaten. Your gold and silver have rusted, and their rust will be evidence against you, and it will eat your flesh like fire. You have laid up treasure for the last days. Listen! The wages of the laborers who mowed your fields, which you kept back by fraud, cry out, and the cries of the harvesters have reached the ears of the Lord of hosts (5:1-4).

These verses are a warning against those who embrace *laissez-faire* capitalism without question and declare that workers should be paid whatever the market value of labor establishes. Those who pay wages determined solely by the law of supply and demand, leaving workers with an unfair share of the profits from their labor, will one day have to face God's judgment and answer for their injustices. Workers created in the image of God must not be exploited.

I know about one American company that manufactured T-shirts in Haiti and paid the women producing the shirts about $5 a day. That $5 a day was considered good wages in Haiti, but considering that each woman made approximately 30 shirts a day and that each shirt sold for about $30 in the United States, you have to conclude that these women weren't getting a fair deal. Don't get me wrong: In a country that has an unemployment rate of well over 66 percent,[3] those women were glad to have their jobs. But the question we Red Letter Christians must ask is whether employers (such as this one) have the right to take advantage of the situation in Haiti and other poor countries to pay their workers less than what biblical fairness requires.

Within our own country we should ask candidates their opinions regarding the fairness of the present minimum wage. If their answer is negative, we should expect to hear from them what each intends to do about it. Some "liberal" states such as Pennsylvania, California and New York have established state minimum wages that are significantly higher than that which has been set in place by the federal government.

Should other states that are fiscally conservative be required by federal law to do what's fair?

Justice is a big thing in the Bible, and there is much written about those in government who do not protect the poor. In Isaiah 10:1-4, we read:

> Ah, you who make iniquitous decrees,
> who write oppressive statutes,
> to turn aside the needy from justice
> and to rob the poor of my people of their right,
> that widows may be your spoil,
> and that you may make the orphans your prey!
> What will you do on the day of punishment,
> in the calamity that will come from far away?
> To whom will you flee for help,
> and where will you leave your wealth,
> so as not to crouch among the prisoners
> or fall among the slain?
> For all this his anger has not turned away;
> his hand is stretched out still.

This is one of many verses that those who make the laws need to consider.

CHAPTER 15

DEBTOR NATION

Because of the war in Iraq, little attention has been given to some of the good things that have happened to the economy during George W. Bush's presidency. Were it not for the cost of the war, our government might be running surpluses close to those accumulated during the Clinton White House. "We are at full employment, and maybe more than full employment" according to some economists.[1] There are some at the Harvard Business School who contend that the federal deficit, strange as it may seem, is not the major threat to our economic future that some of us fear.[2] Nevertheless, there are deep concerns among those same economists that we are not running government surpluses. Much talk abounds concerning our government's inability, even during these prosperous times, to set aside enough money to fund Social Security benefits in the years ahead. There are also those who express concern over our aging population, driving the cost of Medicare-covered health-care out of sight.

With the costs of both Social Security and Medicare looming before us, we should be thinking about the ramifications of all those baby boomers getting ready for retirement. The Bible says much about caring for the widow and the orphan, and Red Letter Christians should be asking if the Church will be able to care for them as the Bible suggests, or if even very politically conservative Christians will face the reality that government dollars must be forthcoming to meet these concerns. If the latter is the answer, we must then wonder where the money will come from—will our government borrow even more from China to cover its obligations?

National Debt

We must consider the political implications of America's indebtedness. Nations can easily translate their accumulations of foreign currency reserves into political power. Consider the situation in 1956, when President Dwight D. Eisenhower wanted to end the invasion of Suez by the British.[3] He simply directed the Federal Reserve to put a run on the British pound and blocked the International Monetary Fund from stabilizing the British currency. He was able to do so because the British owed America so much money. Faced with the prospect of financial collapse, the British withdrew from Suez as Eisenhower wanted.

I wonder how much control China will have over U.S. foreign policies in the years to come—that country now holds more than *a trillion dollars* in U.S. currency reserves.[4] Will our debts force America to execute Chinese foreign policy? At the very least, the fact that they have amassed large amounts of our currency enables the Chinese to keep their currency weak relative to ours, making Chinese goods very inexpensive compared to U.S.-made items in places like Wal-Mart. We have to ask if buying from China is destroying manufacturing jobs for many Americans. There are many who think so.

Argentina is a frightening example of what could happen to America because of our growing indebtedness. In 2001, investors realized that Argentina's debts were too great for that nation to handle, and they called in the loans. Overnight, the value of the Argentinean peso dropped precipitously. Those who had mortgages in U.S. dollars lost their homes, there was a run on the banks and people were soon left without money even to buy food.[5] Keep in mind that this happened in a country with virtually no previous inflation and a 6-percent annual economic growth rate.[6]

A scenario like this should send chills up our spines. And we should refuse to be taken in when we are told by government economists that it could never happen here because "foreigners will continue to provide all the funds we need as long as America remains a good place to invest."[7]

Nation of Debtors

The most important problem that we as a debtor nation should tackle is our individual borrowing from abroad as a result of our seemingly insatiable consumerism. This is a matter seldom discussed by politicians. American longings for iPods, flat screen TVs and a host of other luxury items have led us to borrow from foreign sources without most of us realizing it. We consumers believe we owe money to banks or credit card companies, and don't realize that foreign investors are buying up our debts and mortgages at the rate of $850 billion a year.[8] That amount is equal to the annual output of Brazil, the tenth largest economy in the world, according to Laura Alfaro of the Harvard Business School ("output" refers to the total market value of goods and services produced by a nation).[9] In short, never mind the national debt owed by the government; let's think long and hard about how much individual consumers are in debt to foreign nations.

Perhaps even more disturbing is that mortgage debts have increased so steeply in the last five years that almost $3 trillion has been added to our debt to foreign investors.[10] People have mortgaged their homes to buy cars, swimming pools and new furniture, and to go on vacation or make home improvements. For several years the value of real estate had been soaring, and it seemed reasonable to take out mortgages on homes that had increased in value to pay for such luxuries—and Americans did so without realizing the possible consequences.

As you probably know, many of these mortgages were made with "floating interest rates." As those interest rates have gone up, the monthly payments have also increased dramatically. Many Americans now find themselves unable to make their required payments. Economists point out that banks made loans available to hundreds of thousands of home-buyers who did not have the means to keep up with them. Foreclosures on housing have reached record highs and financial ruin has been the fate of hundreds of thousands of hardworking citizens—and these individual citizens' misfortune has begun to profoundly impact our broader economy. The housing market is deflated and there is a downturn in the construction of new homes. This, in turn, impacts the production and sale of building supplies, furniture and other household merchandise.

Yet instead of encouraging responsible restraint when it comes to personal finances, the message we often hear from our leaders is that it's our responsibility to spend *more*—that the U.S. economy depends on consumers getting out there to shop! When will we realize that we can't spend our way out of debt?

I have no quick fixes to allay the threats our consumeristic lifestyle has created, but I do believe we should look for candidates who understand what we're facing as a nation. It's not likely that those running for Congress or even the presidency will have the economic expertise to answer all of these difficult and urgent challenges, but they should at least be aware of the problems. Those running for national office ought to have some idea how our nation can have a balanced federal budget; we simply can't go on increasing the national debt and have monthly trade deficits in the hundreds of billions of dollars without severe consequences somewhere not too far down the line.

We should also look for candidates who will encourage Americans to be responsible with their personal finances and who will reject the falsehood that "spending more saves more." Might the candidates have some ideas about how we as a culture can reward saving and responsibility rather than overspending and imprudence?

We have come, nationally and individually, a long way from the biblical principle of owing no one anything but love (see Rom. 13:8). While I'm not about to call debt a sin, I must say it is not a good thing for our nation or for us.

CHAPTER 16

WASTEFUL GOVERNMENT

The government needs some major restructuring of the ways it raises and spends money, if it is to do what is needed for the American people. If ours is to be a government of the people and for the people, we must implement some new ideas.

There are a few proposals floating around that deserve attention, especially from Red Letter Christians, that address the issue of government spending. Some of them are modest and others are grandiose. One thing is certain: The government cannot go on doing business as usual. New ideas must be considered. Let's take a look at a few of them.

The Pay-as-You-Go Rule

In March 2007, the Senate Budget Committee passed a resolution to reinstate the pay-as-you-go budget rule, which had been enforced during the 1990s. In simple language, this rule prevents Congress from enacting any new entitlement appropriations or tax legislation that adds to the federal budget deficit. Whenever Congress wants to spend more money on entitlement programs such as Medicare, Medicaid and Social Security, it must first provide the means for funding them. This must be done without borrowing from either the private sector (such as banks) or from foreign nations (such as China and other countries, as we are doing now). The principle of pay-as-you-go especially applies to tax policies, so no tax cuts can be approved without Congress coming up with ways to compensate for the loss of income those cuts might create.

This seems quite reasonable and responsible, but there are some serious concerns to be considered. One of these concerns, raised by the Bush Administration's financial experts, says that this rule, on balance, will harm the economy because it prevents Congress from extending the 2001 and 2003 tax cuts without paying for them. These experts point out that tax cuts can provide stimulants for the nation's economy. They ask that we consider how the tax cuts during the Kennedy Administration helped our national economy by making funds available for investments in businesses and industries. That led not only to increased profits for investors, but it also generated increased employment for workers. Furthermore, the tax cuts during the Kennedy years put more money for spending into the hands of the American people, and their increased spending gave the economy another big boost. People spent more and our industries produced more, and this dynamic put more people to work. Furthermore, the profits made by investors were reinvested, thus creating even more jobs. It's easy to see how this kind of business cycle works, and evidence seems to suggest that it is working well again.

What the Bush Administration's economic advisors fear is that a Democratic Congress and a Democratic president might reverse the Bush tax cuts, and thus cancel out much of the good that has already been accomplished by them. They point out that, as of the summer of 2007, the stock market was booming, unemployment was at 4.5 percent (which is as low as economists say is desirable) and the average American seemed to be doing well.[1] Economists with Goldman Sachs (a huge investment bank based in New York) agree, and they go on to claim that the short-term effects of ending the Bush tax cuts, as the Democrats propose to do, might have grave long-term consequences.[2] These nonpartisan economists argue that the federal deficits created by the tax cuts do not pose as serious a problem as many imagine, and will not necessarily hurt us in the short run. That, they say, is because foreign investors are more than willing to invest in America at the present time because they pay less U.S. taxes by doing so. These investments, Goldman Sachs points out, help stimulate American businesses and industries, creating all kinds of trickle-down effects for the working people of this country.

On the other hand, Federal Reserve Chairman Ben Bernanke warns that the long-term effects of the government's debt and deficits, incurred in part by the tax cuts, could be harmful to the nation.[3] According to Bernanke, these federal deficits will force the government to borrow money away from private American sources (such as banks and insurance companies), leaving less money to be invested in American economic development in the private sector. He also notes that as American corporations borrow from foreign sources money that they need to expand their operations, the profits made by those foreign lenders go overseas. That means that America could, in the long run, gradually grow poorer.

Many different Christian groups have a vested interest in keeping America solvent and fiscally strong. First, Evangelical missiologists rightly point out that American dollars have been of great importance in financing the work of the Church around the world. And while God is not dependent on our U.S. dollars to carry out the evangelistic and social ministries inherent in the Great Commission (see Matt. 28:18-20), there is little doubt that American dollars have sustained much of the work of missions over the past century. If the U.S. economy "goes south," as is predicted by some prophets of doom, there could be serious consequences for the spreading of the gospel around the world.

Second, the Religious Right is especially concerned about what might happen to the American economy because so much of what they have accomplished toward winning the culture wars has been driven by American dollars. Religious talk radio, with its more than 1,500 stations,[4] requires financial contributions that largely come from middle-class Americans who have money to spare. Jim Dobson's program *Focus on the Family*, which has been a dominant influence for the Religious

Right, requires tens of millions of dollars annually to stay on the air.[5] And consider the money required to produce religious television and the hundreds of religious newspapers that promote a very conservative political agenda. Such indispensable weapons in the battle to capture the hearts and minds of America (and as they claim, "to drive back the forces of secularism"[6]) are dependent on the money our economy is able to put into the pockets of politically conservative American Evangelicals.

Third, Red Letter Christians have a vested interest in the American economy because we see the financial resources of our country as a trust from God that should be used to address such needs as ministering to the world's poor and arresting the AIDS pandemic ravaging the developing world. If our nation's financial situation becomes tight, it is unlikely that Americans will respond to needs like these.

So is the pay-as-you-go rule a good measure to limit our government's wasteful spending, or might it damage our economy in the short- or long-term? Red Letter Christians have a responsibility to look at both sides of the argument and evaluate the pros and cons of this rule.

The Line-Item Veto

When a spending bill is presented to a president, he or she is faced with the prospect of having to sign it, even if the bill has attached to it items that waste taxpayer money or serve special-interest groups. Sometimes the items attached to bills include dubious expenditures that some members of Congress have added in order to do favors for people in their home districts. A notable example of this was the request for several hundreds of millions of dollars to build a bridge to an island off the mainland of Alaska.[7] The congressman from that district made no apologies when faced with claims that, while the bridge would create high-paying jobs for people in his district and be an economic boon for many of his constituents, it would serve the transportation needs of a mere handful of people. He was well aware that his attachment was an unnecessary expenditure, but he let those who wanted his vote for the budget know that they had better yield to his demands.

With a line-item veto, a president could veto such questionable "pork barrel projects" while signing into law the rest of what he or she deemed to be necessary funding. That could cut government waste significantly and make more funds available to address that which is most important to Red Letter Christians—namely, meeting the needs of the poor. Without the line-item veto, there will continue to be members of Congress who go on stealing from the public and withholding resources that could help the impoverished widow and orphan. Both former President Clinton and President Bush enthusiastically support the line-item veto because they both know that without it, funding of wasteful programs will continue in bipartisan fashion.

When looking at the potential of a candidate, on the state as well as the federal level, ask whether or not that candidate is ready to make a public commitment to support and perhaps even sponsor a bill that would make line-item vetoes possible.

Faith-Based Initiatives

Picking up on an initiative promoted by his predecessor Bill Clinton, President Bush came up with an answer to both providing government funding for and management of social welfare programs and having faith-based groups (such as churches) finance and run them. Recognizing that faith-based programs are more economical and effective than government-sponsored programs, he developed a plan whereby the government makes funds available to faith-based programs with the stipulation that none of the money be used for religious purposes. That is, if a church sets up a tutoring program, the government may provide funds for the tutoring but not for any religious activities. Religious ministry must be separate from the tutoring, and no government dollars can be used to fund it.

For the most part, the Faith-Based Initiatives program has bipartisan support, hailed by both liberals and conservatives as an effective solution to meeting people's needs. There are some, however, who have raised questions about it. First, there are those who ask if it really is possible to keep the "secular" part of these programs free from strong religious influences. "In the end," they ask, "if the program is held in a church, isn't a religious message communicated by that fact alone? And if those leading the programs are understood to be dedicated members of the church, wouldn't that in and of itself have proselytizing effects? Isn't there a crossing of the line between Church and state inherent in the president's initiative?"

Second, there are those who raise some serious questions about whether or not this program has become too politicized. There are accusations that Karl Rove, President Bush's former chief political strategist, used the Faith-Based Initiatives program to "buy" support for the Republican Party. Some suggest that this has been done, for example, by offering African-American churches money for their social programs on the condition that the pastors of these churches support Republican candidates when it's election time.[8] In Camden, New Jersey, there are African-American congregations who have received significant financial grants, while the largest tutoring program in that city had its application for financial assistance turned down.[9] Could this have been because the leaders of that program were not in tune with the politics of the White House? Whether or not politics played a part in the rejection of that particular tutoring program is hard to say, but there is little doubt that such a situation does raise questions.

Third, and perhaps most pertinent to our consideration of the Faith-Based Initiatives program, is the reality that, while the president promised millions of dollars to fund it, only a fraction of that money has been delivered.[10] David Kuo, a one-time executive on the White

House staff who directed the program, resigned his position and gave this as one of his primary reasons for leaving.[11] Kuo's book, *Tempting Faith*, describes his disillusionment with the White House's Faith-Based Initiatives and received wide coverage in the media, generating much skepticism about the program.

Red Letter Christians need to be on the frontlines of this issue and be fearless about asking whether or not the government should continue funding Faith-Based Initiatives. If we believe in the program, we should ask candidates if they are willing to support it, and if so, how much money they believe should be budgeted for it.

It should be noted that my friend Jim Wallis, the leader of the Call to Renewal movement and editor of *Sojourners* magazine, is very supportive of the Bush Administration's proposals on this matter, though he too raises questions such as those I have cited here.

A Flat Tax

I'm sure that I'll get into a lot of trouble with most of my Red Letter Christian friends when I suggest doing away with the graduated income tax and replacing it with a flat tax.

Put simply, the graduated income tax presently in place means that the more money you make, the greater the proportion of your income has to be paid to the government at tax time. I'm sure that most of you are probably aware that an increase in your income sometimes puts you into a higher tax bracket, meaning that you pay a larger percent of your income to the Internal Revenue Service. With the graduated income tax system, those in low-income brackets pay little in the way of taxes, and those whose incomes fall below a certain government-established level pay nothing at all.

With a flat tax, on the other hand, everyone, rich or poor, would be required to pay the same proportion of his or her income in taxes.

For instance, if the flat tax was 10 percent, then the individual who earned $36,000 a year would pay $3,600 in taxes, while a person who earned $3 million a year would pay the government $300,000.

Let's take a closer look. At first it might seem that low-income people would get a bad deal with the flat tax because they would have to hand over some of their scant earnings to the IRS. However, studies show that, in the end, the flat tax would provide so much more money for the federal treasury that it would then be possible for the government to spend much more to help the poor.[12]

If you are wondering where all the extra money would come from, just consider what's wrong with the present system. Most people know that the tax system now in place has all kinds of loopholes and questionable deductions that rich people, with highly paid tax advisers and lawyers, can use to significantly lower what they pay in income tax. There are rich individuals, as well as multi-million-dollar corporations, that pay little or nothing to the government in taxes because they have legal help that enables them to "work the system" to their advantage. With a flat tax, there would be no more loopholes or questionable deductions.

A flat tax would also mean an enormous cut in government spending, resulting from a dramatic downsizing of the vast Internal Revenue Service bureaucracy, which now costs billions of dollars each year to operate.[13] The IRS would be cut to a mere fraction of its present size because the accounting needed to keep track of tax requisites and receipts would be greatly simplified.

The additional money raised and saved by a flat tax system could fund a program of universal healthcare, covering the 44 million Americans who are presently without health insurance. The government also could have what it needs to sustain Medicare and Medicaid. With this extra money, Social Security could be kept solvent and the array of necessary entitlement programs presently slated to be cut could be kept in place.

Stephen Forbes, the publisher of *Forbes* magazine and one-time candidate for the Republican nomination for the presidency, was the first politician in recent years to seriously propose the flat tax.[14] When he first talked about it, I joined with the scoffers and called it unfair to the poor. But the more I listened to Forbes and considered the facts and figures he used to make his case, the more I leaned toward affirming his proposal. When I further considered how much money the flat tax would save the government and how much greater tax revenues would be, I was completely won over. Granted, there may be some negative consequences forthcoming from a flat tax, but so far I haven't come across any to convince me that Forbes' proposal was a bad idea.

I have some Left-leaning friends who condemn the flat tax as politically conservative dogma, but I contend that America is tired of the doctrinaire politics of the Left and Right, and of the Democratic Party's ideology versus that of the Republican Party. Right now, Americans are looking for pragmatic solutions to our nation's problems. If the flat tax is a workable correction to a system that benefits rich people who know how to work it to their advantage, and if it brings the government more money to meet society's basic needs—especially those of the poor—then I am for it! And my Red Letter Christian brothers and sisters should be for it, too.

A Special-interest Group for the Poor

When asked what she looked for in a candidate, Arianna Huffington, the well-known journalist and political commentator, answered, "I am looking for that person who has the poorest of the poor in mind when policies are developed."[15] She went on to say, "I want to know what a candidate will do for those whom Jesus called 'the least of these.' The rich are able to take care of themselves!" Red Letter Christians want people who think like that to run for office.

Red Letter Christians have a calling to be a special-interest group on behalf of the poor, and to refuse support for candidates who flagrantly waste millions of tax dollars on needless spending. We should lobby members of Congress not with dollars, but by appealing to those values for the common good that are held by most of society and that are strong commitments of Red Letter Christians. To do anything less is to fail in our calling to bring the "principalities and powers" under the lordship of Christ.

THE GOVERNMENT ISSUES

SECTION FIVE

CHAPTER 17

POLITICAL LOBBYISTS

Will Rogers once said, "Nobody should complain about the U.S. Congress. It's the best Congress money can buy!"

Of course, it is wrong to suggest that everyone who goes to Washington to serve in the halls of our government are sold out to special-interest groups. Most of the men and women in Congress I know are people who strive to carry out their duties well and are deeply committed to being persons of integrity. The press highlights those who are corrupt, but they are the exceptions, not the rule. Politics is a noble profession, and there is something wrong when calling someone a politician is being pejorative.

There is a problem with our political system, however, because to run for office—especially on the national level—takes a lot of money, and that reality opens up the possibility that candidates can be unduly influenced by those who contribute to their campaigns. It should not be assumed that all candidates can be bought with campaign contributions, but many are influenced by them.

If you take a good look at who financed a candidate's campaign and how much money was given by those who represent special-interest groups, you are likely to have a fairly accurate measure of how that candidate will vote on many of the bills put on the floor. Special-interest groups, ranging from labor unions to corporations to professional organizations, are more than ready to put money into the campaign coffers of those running for office. Generally (though not always) labor unions give money to Democrats, and corporate interests and professional organizations give money to Republicans. Campaign contributions are given with the expectation that the candidates to whom they are given, should they be elected, will give special attention to the concerns and interests of those who gave the money.

As an example of how this system works, consider the campaign of Collin Peterson, a Democrat in the House who represented the 7th District of Minnesota. In the 2005-2006 election cycle, he received $388,186 from agricultural interests and $106,137 from political action committees.[1] Is it any wonder that he became a prime advocate for a $285 billion farm bill that will funnel subsidies to farmers even when crop prices are high?[2] Furthermore, the subsidies provided by the bill will mostly benefit the largest and richest farmers.[3] Between 2005 and 2006, agricultural businesses spent $44.6 million on political contributions and $193 million on lobbying, according to the non-partisan Center for Representative Politics.[4] Congressman Peterson was one of those whose vote was influenced by that money.

Special Interests in Action

It is easy to become cynical when considering the role campaign financing plays in influencing government. It must be noted, however, that often a special-interest group gives money to a particular campaign fund not to buy that candidate's support, but because he or she already embraces, because of personal conviction, the positions the contributors affirm. On the other hand, there are many ugly examples on both state and national levels of special-interest groups trying to buy the allegiance of would-be legislators.

A friend of mine was upset by the congressman who represented his district when that legislator, to my friend's way of thinking, voted to support bills that were detrimental to poor people while giving big tax breaks to corporate interests. My friend's deep concerns motivated him to run against the incumbent in the next election. He did very well, and there came a point when the polls showed evidence that he was gaining on the incumbent. Suddenly, there was a real possibility that he might actually win.

The teachers' union in this particular district had contributed regularly to the campaign chest of the incumbent congressman, who (up until my friend's campaign) had held what was considered a safe seat in Congress. The union's contributions assured that whenever they had concerns, a call to the office of their congressman would get them an immediate appointment. The teachers' union may not have bought his vote, but they had bought access to him and sympathy for their causes.

As Election Day approached, however, it became impossible to predict which candidate would win. It was then that one of the leaders of the teachers' union called my friend and told him that though they had already given money to his opponent, they also wanted to make a significant contribution to his campaign.

Simply speaking, this union wanted to hedge its bets and ensure they would have access to the halls of Congress regardless which of the two men running was declared the winner. The union leaders were not especially interested in the politics of either man; they only wanted to be sure that they could get a hearing for their agenda.

The union leader who called was somewhat dismayed when my friend questioned him about what motivations lay behind the proffered contribution, and what would be expected in return. Such things are not usually talked about—the expected benefits from contributions are simply implied and assumed.

Personally, I think there's something wrong with a government when money determines who gets heard and who doesn't. What is far more serious, though, is when money buys much more than a hearing for a special-interest group. Consider what happened over a decade ago when Hillary Clinton presented a comprehensive plan for universal health insurance to Congress. (I will not discuss the pros and cons of her plan here, because it was not the virtues or shortcomings of it that determined the plan's eventual defeat.)

Senator Clinton now readily admits that part of the problem was that, back then, she was too new in Washington to understand the political games and the etiquette of Congress. Also not to be discounted when grappling with reasons for the bill's failure are the negative reactions at that time to Hillary Clinton as a person. The forceful manner in which she pushed her healthcare agenda raised the ire of some antifeminist Evangelicals who saw her as the enemy of a tradition that did not support women as strong leaders. Many sermons were preached, questioning leadership roles for women and using Hillary Clinton as an example of a woman who did not know her place.

Beyond any shortcomings Mrs. Clinton might have had, there was big money at work against her and against her proposals for universal health coverage, and these were what ultimately doomed the plan to defeat. First, there was influence bought by campaign contributions from insurance and pharmaceutical corporations, professional medical groups, hospitals and a host of individual doctors. Realizing that the Clintons were determined to pass legislation to significantly change the way they did business, these groups and individuals determined to use their financial resources to line up as many members as possible in the House of Representatives and the Senate to vote according to their interests.

It should be recognized that Democrats controlled both houses of Congress at the time, so blaming Republicans for the defeat of Mrs. Clinton's bill is not an option. Members of her own party joined the opposition. Money, at times, can transcend party loyalties.

Second, the special-interest groups that opposed Clinton's proposals used their money to shape public opinion in very deceptive ways. Insurance companies ran ads in newspapers, on radio and especially on television, communicating that the Clinton plan would establish "socialized medicine" in America, playing on persistent fears about Socialism and Communism. I was amazed at how many ministers, without first studying the proposed healthcare plan, used their influence with the members of their congregations to promote this erroneous belief.

Of course, the Clinton plan was nothing like socialized medicine. Instead, it would have ensured that every American had *privately purchased* health coverage, with the government aiding those who had no access to group policies or were too poor to buy it on their own. But you never would have guessed that from the ads!

I remember one of the most frequently aired commercials at the time told Americans that if the Clinton plan were enacted, the government would determine each person's doctor—people would no longer be able to choose a doctor they personally preferred. That simply was not true! But, as the sociologist W. I. Thomas once said, "When things are real in the imagination, they are real in their consequences,"[5] and the ads deriding the Clinton healthcare plan had people imagining all kinds of things.

Money won the day, both within Washington and without. Special-interest groups used campaign financing to influence Congress in Washington not to support the Clinton plan. Outside Washington, misleading ads molded public opinion so powerfully against the plan that even those members of Congress who had not been recipients of special-interest campaign contributions felt pressured to cave in and vote against it. To go against public opinion was to risk losing in the next election.

In the face of all that money does to control the agenda in Washington, we have to wonder what happened to the "one person, one vote" principle, which is what democracy is all about. Certainly, those who lack financial resources are not able to weigh in on the decision-making process of our government with the effectiveness of those who have the big bucks.

The problem is not only that the medical well-being of Americans was compromised back in the 1990s—it's being compromised *now*.

A prescription medicine (usually referred to as a prescription *drug*) program was recently added to Medicare that means enormous profits for pharmaceutical companies, but has left many poor and elderly people confused and unable to afford the prescriptions required to keep them healthy.[6] Please explain to me how our elected officials have allowed pharmaceutical companies to set the prices of some medicines so high that some people have to choose between buying medicine or buying food. How have those in government allowed an arrangement whereby people who can't afford to buy the medicines they need in the United States make desperate trips across our borders to Canada and Mexico to purchase the same prescriptions at a fraction of the cost?[7] Is it possible that we are seeing what happens when special-interest groups influence the price of prescription medicines via campaign financing?

Today, nearly 47 million Americans, 8.3 million of them children, are without medical insurance.[8] These uninsured people are hardworking Americans who face financial ruin if they, or any member of their families, are hit with a catastrophic medical emergency. That we Christians did not either support the Clinton plan or promote another plan that would provide health coverage for every man, woman and child in this country should be viewed as far more than an embarrassing failure of the Church.

Those who declare that they are pro-life are hypocritical if they do not recognize how providing universal healthcare for the working poor is a pro-life issue. It would be one thing if the rest of the Christian community were like the Amish and chipped in to pay the hospital bills for those who lack health insurance. But we don't! Instead, we stand by the sidelines, shake our heads and say, "Isn't that a shame?"

When it comes to healthcare, to what extent do we feel obligated to live out the lifestyle of the Early Church as described in the book of Acts, wherein Christians met the needs of their brothers and sisters in Christ (see Acts 2:44-45)? Most will agree that few Christians today have the kind of commitment to one another that those first-century Christians had. Few of us are ready to sacrifice for our brothers and sisters in Christ when they are in desperate financial straits, unable to pay for hospital care or medicine.

As we read Galatians 6:10, we should realize that we are not only expected to help our fellow Christians in need, we are also expected to seize every opportunity to help those who are not part of our community of faith. If we do not have the means to do this individually or as a church, we must find some other means of helping those who cannot pay for the medical care they need.

Do you understand why I was disheartened when Christian leaders, who had not studied the Clinton plan for universal healthcare, allowed themselves to be conned by the propaganda of special-interest groups and preached against it? Do you sense something terribly wrong with rejecting the Clinton plan without offering any alternative solution to those unable to pay for adequate medical care?

Jesus made it clear in Matthew 25:43 that not to adequately care for the sick is to turn our backs on Him. In 1 John 3:17-18, we read that we should not bother to talk about having the love of God in our hearts if we are not ready to help brothers and sisters in their hour of need. I think it is fair to say that, given the costs of medical care in today's world, we have to come up with some kind of socially responsible way to pay for the care of the sick. To allow special-interest groups, through campaign financing, lobbying and molding our values through the media, to determine what happens to needy people is to be seduced by the world.

Other Lobbying Concerns

It is a well-known fact that companies in the arms business pour huge amounts of money into lobbying.[9] Most of us are aware that many of these companies employ ex-generals and ex-admirals to rub shoulders with Pentagon officials to ensure that the military establishment keeps buying what they are selling.

According to the White House, the proposed 2008 budget for the military is $481.4 billion, a 62 percent increase since 2001. Total *non-budgeted* spending for the War on Terror from 2001 to 2009 amounts to $661.9 billion. This represents 21 percent of the entire federal budget.[10] Numerous investigations by the Government Accounting Office have produced massive evidence that a great deal of the U.S. defense budget is funneled toward unnecessary spending that does not contribute to making the military stronger or more efficient.[11]

Consider how much money is "stolen" when companies that do business with the Pentagon overcharge (for items such as $640 toilet seats[12]) or increase expenses far beyond what was originally agreed on when they got their government contracts.[13] What is worse is that, while billions of dollars are misappropriated, there is insufficient spending to meet the needs and ensure the safety of men and women in uniform who face combatants on the battlefield. We all have heard reports of inadequate body armor provided for American soldiers who patrol the streets of Baghdad. In newspapers and on television, there are reports of how our military personnel are forced to venture out in vehicles that are not properly equipped to protect them from roadside bombs. We are outraged by reports of the horrendous conditions and inadequate healthcare provided for returning combatants at Walter Reed Hospital in our nation's capital. These men and women who have sacrificed so much to defend our country deserve much better!

It is not that there are insufficient funds to do what is right for those who defend our country. Rather, it is *how* that money is spent that causes such obscenities.

The blame for these immoral and wasteful expenditures cannot be laid solely at the feet of those who run the Department of Defense. Most of the blame must be placed on Congress. The House and Senate are responsible to oversee expenditures for military purposes. But here again, we see the effects of campaign financing. Companies that do business with the government know how to reap benefits by investing in candidates running for office.

Shouldn't we find out whether or not particular contractors have purchased influence with certain members of Congress by making campaign contributions? Shouldn't we ask how some defense contractors are getting away with over-charging and defrauding the government?

What is going on in Iraq right now, as it pertains to the spending of taxpayer dollars, should have us all in a state of outrage. Halliburton, the company for which Vice President Dick Cheney once served as a top executive, has been given contracts worth billions of dollars to assist in the rebuilding of that war-torn country. Not only were these contracts given without competitive bids (in itself legally suspect), they were also given with very few controls on how the money was to be spent.[14] To date, billions of dollars have disappeared, and Halliburton is unable to give any account of where that money has gone.[15]

Why haven't there been Congressional investigations to call the executives of this company to account? Have campaign gifts played a part in the failure of Congress to stop the fiscal abuse of this company?

And what about the rising costs of gasoline? Please don't blame this on the Arabs and OPEC. The fact is, as Wall Street experts point out, an abundance of crude oil is presently available.[16] The shortage of gasoline, which some corporate special-interest groups say is responsible for the rising prices, is the result of a multiplicity of factors. These interests readily point to the Chinese and say that their booming economy is gobbling up gasoline at an incredible rate.[17] That may be true, but the main problem is a shortage of oil refineries right here in America. No new refineries have been built in the United States since 1976.[18] It's not that the oil companies lack the funds to build new refineries—stock market figures show that these companies continue to make astronomically high profits. Don't we have to ask ourselves why our elected officials, who are supposed to look after our interests, aren't doing something to address this problem? We are certainly concerned, so why aren't they?

Obviously, if we are going to have the kind of government that lives up to the principles of justice as defined in Scripture, the system of financing campaigns has to be changed, which is addressed in the next chapter. The present system does not serve the interests of the poor and forgotten people of America, or the oppressed of the world.

CHAPTER 18

CAMPAIGN FINANCE

A Quixotic Campaign

In 1976, I ran for the U.S. Congress. I was an anti-war candidate (which, I suppose, is a dead giveaway of my political leanings). I launched my campaign in the spring of 1974, at the tail end of the Vietnam War, and by the time the primary election was over, so was the war. That, of course, took the wind out of my campaign sails, but along with my volunteers, I continued to work hard right up until Election Day.

The campaign was a learning process for me, and what I discovered about how politics works proved to be both exciting and fascinating. I was fortunate in that, at the time, I was a faculty member at both the University of Pennsylvania and at what is now Eastern University. Anti-war sentiment ran high at both of these schools and I was able to recruit scores of students to join my campaign. These enthusiastic young people were invaluable. They delivered campaign flyers and brochures door to door, which saved a huge amount of money that otherwise would have been spent on mailings. They handled much of the office work at Campaign Headquarters (housed on the front porch of my home). They were available to hand out sample ballots at the polls on the day of the primary. They provided free photography, conducted campaigning by phone, put up "Campolo for Congress" signs and posters from one end of the congressional district to the other, developed position papers on the pressing issues of the day, set up well more than a hundred "coffees" and rallies, and helped with the development of an overall campaign strategy.

These activists, whose commitments to issues such as ending racism, sexism and the destruction of the environment, came on board with me because I shared their political values. Yet occasionally I had to rein in some of the more zealous campaigners because their tactics verged on being unethical. For instance, I was driving home for dinner one evening through a torrential rainstorm and listening to some music on the car radio, when the disc jockey surprised me by saying, "The Campolo for Congress rally scheduled for this evening had to be cancelled due to inclement weather."

As I did not have a rally on my schedule, I called the campaign office to ask why I had not known about such an important event. A young volunteer told me it was because no such rally had been planned. When he saw the storm break loose, he had called every radio station in the Philadelphia area and asked that a public service announcement be made to publicize the cancellation of a rally that had never been planned in the first place. "Fifteen different stations talked about the Campolo for Congress campaign at least four or five different times tonight while people were driving home," he said. "Tony, we could never buy that kind of publicity!"

Of course, I explained to him why what he had done wasn't right and why he should never do such a thing again, but I think this story gives you some idea of the boundless ingenuity and enthusiasm the Campolo for Congress campaign had going for it.

Over the years, as a preacher and a speaker, I had been extensively involved in the activities of the churches throughout my congressional district. I had spoken at everything from church bowling banquets to denominational retreats, so people knew me. And when my candidacy was announced, dozens called the campaign office to volunteer. I had the kind of help that most candidates would have had to pay a small fortune to hire.

My campaign manager, Bill Sabitino, was a Roman Catholic priest who took a leave of absence from his Norbertine order to work with me without pay. His assistant, Paul Daffinee, who was one of my former students, also served for free, out of personal commitment to the principles of the campaign.

Handling the press was my wife, Peggy. Though she had no previous experience at such an assignment, she is an excellent writer and did brilliantly, with the help of Alan Peck, our volunteer photographer. There were more than 30 weekly newspapers in the district and every week I could count on most of them carrying a story, usually with a photo, promoting my candidacy. Each Sunday that I preached anywhere in the district, Peggy was there. On the way home, she would interview me on some hot issues and then write up an article for the papers. Those articles always began by stating where and when I had preached and then went on to clarify, "As is his custom, Dr. Campolo said nothing related to politics or his campaign during his sermon, but in an interview afterward, he said . . ." Then Peggy would add whatever it was I had to say on matters concerning the voters in the district. My pro-war opponent, an honest and hardworking incumbent, was beside himself (by his own admission), because of the extensive newspaper coverage my campaign received.

Any hope of winning against an incumbent in Congress supposedly requires at least half a million dollars to finance the campaign. Having to raise such a vast sum of money is what makes candidates ready to take money from special-interest groups, even with all the pitfalls that have already been discussed.

The Campolo for Congress campaign, however, was run for less than $20,000. I limited donations to $50 per person. Having become concerned about how campaigns are funded, I wanted to make sure that no special-interest group could lay claim to me. It was obvious that $50 would not be enough to buy any candidate.

My campaign was wonderfully effective, in spite of the fact that we raised comparatively little money. Our funds were miniscule compared to what is generally required and expected in politics. Such a campaign was possible because I was in a unique position to recruit volunteers. Typically, it is not possible to do as much campaigning as we did with so little money.

I lost! But there was very little disappointment at the election-night party. The registration in the district was 7 to 1 Republican, and as an "independent" Democrat, I did far better than any of the political pundits had imagined or predicted. I had put a scare into the opposing camp and, more important, had used the campaign to raise a host of issues that needed to be discussed by the general public.

Among those issues was campaign financing.

Reforming the System

The issue of campaign financing is seldom brought up when Christians discuss politics or write books about their political concerns. Yet, as I described in the previous chapter, how campaigns are financed may be *the* issue that needs addressing if justice is to be done in government. We cannot grasp why members of Congress to whom we present our biblically based concerns do not always readily support us if we do not understand the pressures put on them by special-interest groups that provide money to help get them elected.

Right after the scandal that brought down the Nixon Administration, a host of campaign reforms were passed into law. Those in Congress at the time were afraid to oppose any legislation aimed at reform because public sentiment was so incensed over the fallout from the Watergate affair. Any opposition to reform would have cost candidates dearly in upcoming elections. Consequently, reform became the order of the day. Caps were put on the size of contributions candidates could receive from individual donors. Means were created to provide some government financing for candidates running for the presidency. These were designed to diminish the need for them to become beholden to special-interest groups. Restraints were put on lobbying.

At first, it looked as though the new system would work, but the devil is in the details, as they say. Within a few years, loopholes were found in the new laws, and special-interest groups found ways to do what they had always done: use money to help candidates get elected.

It would take another entire book to explain the reforms that were put into place and the clever ways those who want to circumvent the law have found to get around them, but the most common technique is to put money into a newly created organization that declares itself to be non-partisan and supportive of no particular candidate. Then the money is used, via television and other media ads, to raise issues or stories to discredit the opponent targeted for defeat.

Another way of getting around the intentions of the reform laws is for a wealthy candidate to put his or her own money into a campaign, rather than accepting any contributions. While this arrangement frees the candidate from undue influence from any special-interest group, it certainly gives an advantage to rich candidates over those of more modest means. The intention of the campaign reform bills was to create a level playing field for all the candidates, but financing one's own campaign has become one way of evading the spirit of those reforms. There should be limits placed on how much candidates can contribute to their own campaigns for office.

I would like to see an arrangement that limits what can be *spent* on campaigns. To my way of thinking, this would mean public financing. I believe that there should also be regulations limiting the *length* of political campaigns. As it is now, the seemingly endless duration of campaigns drives up the cost of running for public office in ways that stagger the imagination—not to mention exhausting the electorate.

Right now, there is a new array of proposals that, if enacted into law, would go a long way toward making the process of running for office less susceptible to manipulation by special-interest groups and more available to those who aren't rich.

A Referendum for Reform

Political scientists who have studied campaign and election practices do not see much possibility for change.[1] This is because those who have power to reform the system have little desire to change the process that got them elected in the first place. But my son, Bart, has a rather unique proposal to overturn this dynamic. He suggests that we petition to have a referendum put on the ballot that calls for specific reforms in the laws governing elections. This would take reform out of the hands of those who have a vested interest in keeping things as they are and put the power to change the system in the hands of the general public. I know some brilliant political science professors, and all of them say that my son's proposal is one of the few ways to achieve election reform that might actually work.

What if we Red Letter Christians started such a petitioning effort? Working together toward such a goal might be the kind of activity that could galvanize a movement and draw support to our cause. Our efforts to bring about election reform would have to be non-partisan, because true election reform is not something that favors one party over another. Rather, reform should create a more just and open election process that benefits all Americans. Becoming involved in such an effort would certainly be one way for us Red Letter Christians to live out our commitment to serve the common good.

There is still another way to overcome the problems campaign financing has created for the American election process, a solution that proved viable during Pat Robertson's campaign for the Republican Party nomination for the presidency. Robertson ran an effective campaign that escaped being held hostage to any special-interest group, and we should give serious consideration to his approach.

Undoubtedly, the high visibility of Robertson through his *700 Club* television show gave him the kind of name recognition that would be an asset for any candidate. But there was more to his campaign than that, which caused people to take his run for president seriously and had nothing to do with money. The effectiveness of Robertson's campaign was directly related to his ability to win over a large segment of the Evangelical community by appealing to their longing for a politics marked by spiritual values and their desire to have religion play a vital role in determining the future of our nation. Many Christians across the nation—and many in the early-caucus state of Iowa—responded to his call to bring God into national political discussions and to establish America as a nation built on biblical principles.

Without commenting on Robertson's view of what America should be like politically, it's easy to see that he demonstrated the possibility of staging an effective campaign without becoming beholden to any special-interest groups. He proved that a credible run for the presidency was possible without selling out.

I am sure what Robertson did could be done by a Red Letter Christian, mobilizing another grassroots movement that circumvents the established, money-controlled election system. Of course, the political agenda would be very different from the one espoused by Robertson—as well as the vision for what role Christian faith should play in determining America's future—but there is little doubt in my mind that such a leader could show Americans an alternative to the ways money influences political decision-making. He or she would make every effort to transcend partisan politics and overcome the divide that polarizes the Religious Right and the Religious Left, which would have a special attraction for young people who are tired of typical politicians and want to march to the beat of a different drummer. This leader would make caring for the poor a dominant political concern, hitting a responsive chord in the hearts and minds of Christians in all walks of life.

In the desperate need for election reform and a new way of funding political campaigns, I see an opportunity for Red Letter Christians to work for change and impact America with the values of the Kingdom of God.

CHAPTER 19

THE RIGHT KIND OF CANDIDATE

The Bible says that without dreamers and visionaries, people perish (see Prov. 29:18). As we face the political challenges of our times, we need visionaries as our candidates. We ought to look for men and women who dare to point Americans away from our self-centered, consumeristic values so that we might be a light on a hill, modeling something of God's Kingdom here on earth. We should ask which candidates best communicate the kind of vision articulated by Martin Luther King, Jr., when he stood on the steps of the Lincoln Memorial and gave his famous "I Have a Dream" speech. That was a vision that motivated America to strive for biblically prescribed human unity, and invited us to live out the values written into the Declaration of Independence—affirming that "all men are created equal" and that they "are endowed by their Creator with certain inalienable rights."

The Hebrew prophets were visionaries in that same spirit, men who envisioned the world as God wanted it to be—a world of peace and well-being. Consider Zechariah's vision of a transformed society:

> Old men and old women shall again sit in the streets of Jerusalem, each with staff in hand because of their great age. And the streets of the city shall be full of boys and girls playing in its streets (Zech. 8:4-5).

Tragically, we live in a time when the elderly in our cities are afraid to leave their houses at night and children are not safe when they play in the streets. But like the prophet Zechariah, we long for a day when old folks can lean on their canes as they sit on the front steps of their homes in our American cities, to watch children playing carefree on sidewalks and streets.

In that same chapter, Zechariah gives us a vision of a society that is such a compelling model of *shalom* that "the inhabitants of many cities" come to see its example of what God intends for all cities and nations (vv. 20-21). With the prophet, we envision a time when the peoples of the earth will take hold of our sleeves and say, "Let us go with you, for we have heard that God is with you" (v. 23).

America seems to have lost its way in seeking to be humanity's best hope for the future. There was a time when government did not make lying official policy (euphemistically calling it "disinformation"), when military interrogators did not torture their prisoners, when soldiers did not die in vain, and when our need for security did not allow for spying on our citizens unless there was due process of law. We are hungry for that kind of America again, and we should seek out candidates who believe we can make that kind of America again.

So we should ask ourselves, Does the candidate under consideration promote divisive politics that secures votes by setting groups against each other? Is he or she a candidate who seeks to get elected by playing races against one another, or by catering to homophobic fears, or by appealing to religious prejudices by focusing on only a few issues and excluding others? Stay away from any such candidate, and work for their defeat.

Rejecting Self-centered Politics

Americans have been fed a constant diet of fear since 9/11. We have been seduced into being primarily concerned about electing people we believe can keep us safe. We look for candidates who promise to kill off our enemies, thereby giving us a sense of security. This is not to say that national security is unimportant, but a politics guided by fear has made us into a paranoid people who are blind to the magnificent things we can do for our own citizens and for the people of the world. Rather than voting based on fear, we should instead choose candidates who fearlessly believe that we can create a better and more peaceful world, and who have the nerve to launch the great enterprises for humanity that a great American people are ready to forge.

The '60s were tumultuous times, but for all of their upset they were years when many Americans were alive with dreams and visions, rather than governed by their fears. In those days, Americans believed they could move toward a world without poverty, war and injustice. When Richard M. Nixon and John F. Kennedy vied for the presidency, each challenged America to realize its potential for great achievements.

Then came the '70s, which some social critics have called the "Me Decade." It was a time when Americans largely turned from their altruistic impulses and gave into self-centered desires. More and more, we became a people who wanted from government only that which would serve our self-interests. Materialistic gratifications increasingly dominated our motivations and, for too many of us, those gratifications were the only things that mattered.

This egoism continued with us into the '90s, and we saw it when Bill Clinton ran against then-President George H. W. Bush. During one event structured like a New England town-hall meeting, those in the audience were given the opportunity to ask questions of the two candidates. One young man asked a question that greatly disturbed me. "I'm 21 years old," he said. "This year will be the first time I get to vote in a presidential election. What I want to know is what each of you would do for me, should either of you be elected."

I was dismayed as both Bush and Clinton competed to promise that young man, as well as the national audience, benefits each would deliver for young voters. As I listened, I considered how far we Americans had moved from John F. Kennedy's powerful inaugural speech in which he challenged us to "ask not what your country can do for you . . . ask what you can do for your country!" The shift from a politics that challenged Americans to live out their altruistic impulses to a politics of self-interest was all too evident in that moment.

To counteract this downward, self-seeking spiral, we ought to seek candidates who call Americans to higher ideals. Those we elect should inspire us to live generously rather than selfishly, and they should be determined to create a world where all men and women have the freedom to work for the common good.

Red Letter Christians should *not* understand freedom as the right to do whatever we want, so long as we don't interfere with the rights of others. Instead, we must view freedom as liberation from forces that hinder us and others from becoming all God wills for each of us as part of the Kingdom. To be a Red Letter Christian is to embrace a politics that ensures every human being the freedom to actualize his or her God-given potential and purpose in life. This means that we evaluate candidates not just in terms of what they can do for us, but also in terms of what they can do to offer each and every American the education and opportunity needed to prepare for his or her aspired vocation. We should ask ourselves which candidates have worked out viable plans for creating safe and secure environments that are essential for children to grow up to their purpose, according to the will of God.

Being Born Again Is Not Enough

American politics is an anomaly to Europeans. On the other side of the Atlantic, religion is seldom paraded by candidates. This contrasts with the U.S., where candidates on both sides of the political aisle recognize that there are votes to be gleaned from certain segments of the electorate if voters can identify with the religious commitments of those running for office. To that end, there is a great deal of religious posturing that goes on before elections.

Evangelicals tend to put great stock in candidates who give evidence that they have had born-again experiences and who declare themselves a part of our spiritual community. To further a candidate's standing among Evangelicals, it is common practice to publish a book or two that appears on the shelves of Christian bookstores, delving into the spiritual experiences and practices of that candidate.

Legend has it that some members of clergy visited Abraham Lincoln at the White House to assure him that fighting and winning the Civil War was God's will. Lincoln is said to have answered, "My concern is not whether God is on our side; my greatest concern is to be on God's side, for God is always right."

That kind of humility is fitting for those who hold public office. To be so arrogant as to declare one's decisions on political matters synonymous with God's will, just because one is born again, is close to idolatry. I say "close," because there may be some decisions that appear so biblically prescribed that they can be made with some degree of certainty. But even then, one must speak with caution, because reading the Bible is an exercise in interpretation. There have been times when Christians have interpreted the Bible wrongly, as when many once thought Scripture clearly supported slavery. Just because a candidate prays for direction does not mean the decisions that follow are the will of God.

A particular candidate might have a deep personal faith and a clean personal morality, but that candidate might make decisions on the societal level that do harm for the poor and oppressed of the nation and the world. They then do great evil. It may be that a non-Christian candidate espouses political commitments on crucial social issues that are more in line with what the Bible teaches than does a deeply religious, born-again opponent. If we are honest, we will admit that there are many who believe in Christ and maintain a regular devotional life but who may be more guided by party allegiances than biblical values when it comes to government policy. Sometimes those whose personal morality is above reproach fail to take political positions that are in accord with the red letters in the Bible.

As a case in point, recall the shocking fact that many of those in Nazi Germany who supported Hitler were committed church members, deemed "good" by their fellow countrymen. Consider that well into the twentieth century, there were sincere, born-again Christians who supported racist policies that perpetuated segregation. Even more recently, some of the most intensely committed Christians in South Africa supported racial apartheid and saw in Nelson Mandela the incarnated spirit of the anti-Christ. Sincerely religious people can promote great wrongs.

I don't want to put down the significance of public declarations of faith that so many candidates make to their voting constituencies. Faith commitments are of *great* importance. A candidate who regularly prays and considers, in light of Scripture, how controversial issues should be decided is a comfort for fellow believers. There will always be cynics who raise questions about how sincere such candidates are in their religious declarations, but many of us are encouraged to learn that certain candidates take God seriously and look for divine guidance when making political decisions.

What concerns me is the tendency to consider a declaration of faith enough to convince us that such candidates deserve our votes. That a person seeks God's will is no assurance that he or she will find it. When making decisions, there are many influences that enter in. Isn't that true for each of us? How many times do we, even after praying, find ourselves in a quandary, trying to determine whether what we feel we ought to do is really God's will or a misguided and disguised version of our own will?

The Necessity of Integrity

Do not take what is said here as minimizing the importance of personal morality in the lives of those who hold positions of political power. We need go no further in the Bible than the kings of Israel to see that personal morality has a great impact on what happens to a nation. This reality can be found in the rule of King David: His moral failures on the personal level had disastrous consequences for Israel and greatly hurt David's ability to serve his people. Let it be said, loud and clear, that the integrity of a candidate's personal life has a great deal to do with how that candidate will function in public life.

If corruption in government is to be eliminated, then candidates with good character must be put into office. Government corruption has led far too many Americans to be increasingly skeptical about politics. Crony-ism, payoffs and socially destructive partisanship seem endemic among those who have been given political trust. I, for one, do believe that most politicians try hard to be honest and endeavor to serve the country well, but the corruption of some, especially when they are in the highest places in government, undermines public confidence in all who hold elected office. When citizens lose confidence in those who were elected to lead us, America becomes less stable and the ability of government to do good is greatly lessened. Thus, the matter of a candidate's honesty and integrity deserves intense scrutiny.

"Not to Decide Is to Decide"

When you step into the voting booth, there is a strong probability that none of the candidates on the ballot will fit your exact prescription for someone who embodies *everything* you believe about the important moral issues being considered in the election. But as French philosopher Jean-Paul Sartre once said, "Not to decide is to decide." In politics, as in poker, you have to play with the cards you are dealt. It is not an option to do as many Christians have done and simply walk away from politics.

If we cannot find enough candidates dedicated to the values we hold dear, it may be that it is up to people like you and me to recruit persons we can trust. We may have to go after gifted people who have the values and character we believe elected officials should possess, and press them to take on the task of running as candidates.

We have had too many leaders who have been Machiavellian pragmatists. It was that kind of leadership that led the U.S. to overthrow a democratically elected government in Iran in 1953, to put in place a regime favorable to American foreign policies.[1] That decision, made by the president of the United States, was primarily responsible for poisoning the attitudes of Iranians against an America they labeled "The Great Satan." A decision made by another of our presidents led to the overthrow of a democratically elected government in Chile in 1973, thus creating fears and animosities toward our country that persist to this day throughout Latin America.[2] Justice is a concept with far-reaching implications, and we should elect those who will be far-sighted in promoting it with integrity.

To refuse to be involved in the decision-making processes on Election Day is to let others make moral decisions that impact not only our nation but also the world. Voting is an absolute necessity for Red Letter Christians. If the options are such that none of the candidates can be supported with a clear conscience, then "writing in" a candidate not on the ballot may be a way to express our convictions.

As we were reminded in chapter 1, the British political pundit Edmund Burke once said, "All that is necessary for evil to triumph is for good men to do nothing." It is irresponsible to not be involved in politics. This is a primary arena wherein we have the opportunity to work out our understanding of biblical principles, testing our faith and causing our minds to struggle with the ambiguities of the real world.

Think through the issues! Reflect on how Scripture informs you about the concerns facing voters! Probe the characters of the candidates! Not voting will only make you a victim of what others decide. If this book encourages you to participate in the decision-making processes of coming elections, writing it will have been worth the effort.

CONCLUDING PERSPECTIVES

CHAPTER 20

ON EARTH AS IT IS IN HEAVEN

Often I am asked, "How did you get the way you are? You preach like a true Evangelical, yet when you express your political views, you come across as a social liberal."

That question always challenges me to reflect back on the people and situations that have molded my worldview over the past 50 years. It took a long time for me to change from being what today would be called a "Religious Right advocate" into someone who, while still being theologically conservative, has embraced socially progressive ideas.

My journey began back when I pastored some small but wonderful churches. I started pastoring when I was just 20 years old, and during those very early years of ministry, I was the kind of political conservative Rush Limbaugh would have loved. In those days, I was committed to making America a Christian nation, and was suspicious about the liberal leanings of my own American Baptist denomination, as well as the National Council of Churches and the World Council of Churches. In part, this was because I believed reports I had read in *Readers' Digest* and heard from some of my favorite preachers that all three of these organizations were cozy with socialistic thinking and imbued with liberal theology.[1]

The significant changes in my thinking began to occur during the late '60s and early '70s, when I moved from the pastorate to academia. I was fortunate to get appointments to both Eastern Baptist College (now Eastern University) and the University of Pennsylvania, a prestigious Ivy League school. The students at both of these schools were intensely engaged in the great social movements of the times. Martin

Luther King, Jr., had captivated their hearts and minds as he pled with America to stop living in contradiction to the lofty values set forth in the Declaration of Independence and the Constitution; and William Sloan Coffin had challenged this increasingly counter-cultural generation to oppose the war in Vietnam.

As a professor of sociology, there was no way I could escape dealing with these issues in my classroom discussions. And without question, those discussions changed my thinking. My students raised questions that forced me to rethink and re-evaluate everything that, up until that time, I had neatly systemized and packaged into what I thought was a "Christian worldview." For the first time, I saw my nationalism as a pseudo-religion that kept me from understanding what I began to realize were basic to Christian ethics.

For me, the first major shift into a new thought paradigm came with the civil rights movement. As my politically conservative church friends ranted and raged against Martin Luther King, Jr., and endeavored to justify the prevailing social order, my students challenged me to face up to the teachings of Scripture, which call for an obliteration of all barriers to social equality. I could no longer deny that, in accord with Galatians 3:28, we are called to affirm a new humanity in which people of different races, genders and social classes are made one. There was no question left in my mind that what God wills for us in Christ is what God wills for everyone.

I was more than surprised when some of the Christians I knew, for whom I had the deepest respect, questioned what was obvious to me as biblical precept, and condemned King and the movement for racial equality he led. Their political ideology kept them from embracing what I believed was biblically prescribed justice.

As the civil rights movement called me to challenge the entrenched racist practices of American society, the war in Vietnam escalated. Again my students' questions confronted my assumptions, driving me to inquire what lay behind the political rhetoric that called Americans to support the war, and then to decide if the facts justified our military action in the former French colony. I was disturbed when I discovered that the leaders of my country had not kept their promises to guarantee a free election in Vietnam in 1948 because they were aware that in such an election, Ho Chi Minh, a communist, would have easily won.[2] There was further disillusionment when I learned that my country did not want to abide by the Geneva Accord of 1954, which guaranteed the people of Vietnam the right to determine their own destiny.[3] As the horrors of the war became increasingly well known, questions about the morality of U.S. activities in Vietnam put me in a state of extreme upset. My students did not let up, and it was only a matter of time before I became an anti-war activist.

At the University of Pennsylvania, I organized what must have been one of the most unusual war protest rallies ever. While students were staging disruptive sit-ins and even vandalizing buildings on other campuses, students at U of Penn held an interfaith "pray-in" on the grass of the university commons.

At Eastern College, where I also taught, students joined me in a 15-mile protest march into the heart of Philadelphia. There, we gathered at a large Society of Friends meeting house to pray for peace and listen to several religious leaders from the Philadelphia area speak about our obligations as Christians to oppose the war.

In the fields of sociology and education, what I experienced through those years is called *praxis*. Praxis is the theory of learning that proposes that our actions condition our thinking every bit as much as our thinking influences our actions. It is the belief that intellectual reflection in the context of *doing* molds our consciousness. My reflection in the context of action through the civil rights movement and even more as part of the anti-war movement led me to think differently about my faith in relationship to politics.

My Continued Learning Curve: SPEAK

Since those early days in my teaching career, I have continued to be impacted by students, especially by those who are ready to turn their faith into action. For almost a decade, I have been a strong supporter of an Evangelical group of British students called SPEAK, who have raised issues that I might otherwise have ignored. The questions they are presently asking have sensitized me to some international issues that I strongly believe should be raised in the minds of Christians everywhere.

Right now, members of SPEAK are working hard to help the poor in developing countries by pressing the British government to enact fair trade policies. They point out that the rules and regulations that govern international trade unjustly favor rich industrialized nations to the detriment of the poorer nations of the world.

What I am learning from these students about the unfairness of trade arrangements leads me to believe that fair trade should be an American political issue, taken on by Red Letter Christians. Standing up for fair trade practices is controversial, to say the least. But not to understand how the trade policies our government presently supports impoverish people in developing nations is to fail to work for God's justice in the commercial world.

Both former President Clinton and President Bush are advocates of what are called *free* trade policies. Simply speaking, these policies propose that, in so far as it is possible, countries should not establish protective tariffs that drive up prices of imported goods. For example, if a Chinese company wants to sell a product in our country at a lower cost than the price established by an American company that produces the same product, the U.S. cannot tax the Chinese import such that the price of their product is driven so high that they cannot compete with ours. Conversely, if the U.S. wants to sell American-made computer software in Germany, the government in Berlin cannot establish taxes on our U.S. imports that make our software non-competitive on the German market.

This all seems fair and square to those of us who believe in a free enterprise system that allows for open competition in the marketplace. After all, doesn't the competition of free enterprise ensure that we get the best products at the lowest prices? If a foreign manufacturer can produce a better product at a lower price than what is made in one's own country, doesn't it serve the buyers' interests to keep government from interfering by enacting protective tariffs?

What at first seems fair looks a lot more like injustice when we get a fuller picture of what actually goes on in the world. Let's look at agricultural products as an example. We have already noted how special-interest groups in the agricultural business finance the campaigns of certain members of Congress, and how American farmers are subsidized by billions of dollars each year. Yet the governments of most developing nations do not have the financial means to subsidize their farmers as we are able to do for ours. What this means for many of these poorer countries is that subsidized American farm products can be imported and sold there at prices lower than those set by their own farmers. In some places, American wheat, rice and cotton can be sold at prices so low that farmers in those poor countries are driven out of business. And when we consider that most developing nations are not industrialized, it becomes clear that hurting farmers in those places is an unmitigated injustice. Thousands of poor farmers, who have very few alternative income options, are being driven out of business every year.[4]

Given such realities, many young people show up at the gatherings of the World Trade Organization and call for *fair* trade to replace *free* trade in international commerce. Fair trade, these students say, would allow a poor country to set up protective tariffs to drive up the price of imported products and give goods and commodities produced by indigenous people a chance to compete. At the same time, fair trade would prohibit the establishment of import taxes by rich nations (such as the United States), which make it difficult for developing nations to sell their products in those wealthier countries.

Advocates of fair trade also want to deal with huge corporations that are able, by virtue of their vast buying power, to control the price of coffee beans produced by small farmers in places such as Costa Rica. Ten years ago, coffee farmers were able to make $7 a day. Today their income is down to half that amount.[5] Many people across our country are refusing to patronize coffee shops that do not sell fair trade coffee, produced by farmers who were paid a fair price for their beans.

The SPEAK student movement in the United Kingdom, which first got me to consider the fair trade issue, has now spread to the U.S. They have established a dynamic chapter at Eastern University, where I am a professor emeritus. This chapter of SPEAK has done amazing things through peace movements in Northern Ireland and in the Holy Land, and recently they have worked to improve relationships between Christians and Muslims right here in the United States. Those efforts have led them to raise concerns about how our government relates to our Islamic community, even as it seeks to ensure security for all Americans. Their concerns have become my concerns. Once again, my students have become my teachers.[6]

Thoughts on the Patriot Act

This leads me to some unsettling questions about the Patriot Act that do not lend themselves to easy answers. This act of Congress, initiated at the request of the Attorney General and signed into law by President Bush in October 2001, is viewed by many liberals as a violation of the Bill of Rights. Most conservatives, on the other hand, deem the Patriot Act as absolutely essential to protect America in the midst of the war on terrorism.

Among the objections to the Patriot Act is the claim that it allows for unconstitutional invasions of privacy. Under the Act, the government is authorized to spy on U.S. citizens by wire-tapping their electronic communications without a court order.[7] As presently practiced, this spying creates a sense that "Big Brother" is listening, even on personal conversations. Federal law enforcement can instruct U.S. postal workers to report any persons receiving suspicious mail,[8] the kind of thing we would expect only in totalitarian countries. Perhaps most disturbing is that, under the Patriot Act, our government is able to hold people indefinitely in secret prisons without being charged, without having access to proper legal counsel and without their families knowing where they are.[9]

I was especially disturbed when I learned that government agents have been spying in Islamic mosques.[10] This is an eerie echo of the spying policies of the Soviet Union when that collection of states was governed by a totalitarian communist regime, or even those of North Korea's present government. You were probably horrified when you learned that Christians visiting churches in those places reported government spies at every worship service, and how Christians could be arrested if anything was said or done that might be interpreted as politically subversive.

I wonder if U.S. freedom of religion, guaranteed under the First Amendment of the Constitution, is threatened by the Patriot Act. Will the government next spy on preachers in Christian churches, checking on sermons to see if criticism of U.S. policies, such as those connected with the war in Iraq, might be deemed subversive? Fredrick Nietzsche, the atheist and existentialist, once said something that is good for Red Letter Christians to consider: "Be careful, lest in fighting the dragon you become the dragon." In fighting totalitarian enemies—which radical terrorists certainly are—will *we* become totalitarian?

The retorts to questions raised by those who challenge the Patriot Act coalesce around the basic theme that the "War on Terror" is different from any war our country has fought before. The framers of the Constitution, we are told, never could have envisioned what we Americans now face. Some high-up officials in Washington even say that, in light of present circumstances, it may be time to revise the Bill of Rights.[11] They say that we cannot afford to deal with terrorists only after they have committed their heinous crimes. Instead, we must find out who they are and deal with them *before* they are allowed to carry out their acts of terror. The lives of thousands of people may be at stake, and this reality leads the government to defend policies that go against established rules and practices. As a pertinent example, torture has been considered an obscenity under past U.S. policy, but what if torturing a terrorist enables the government to obtain information that might save lives?

What is strangest to me is that Christians usually decry situational ethics. We often say the absolutes of right and wrong should never be violated. Yet in the present climate of fear in our country, some of us are ready to accept situational ethics as a regrettable but necessary *modus operandi*. This is incredibly inconsistent. Perhaps we should own up to our tacit agreement with Ralph Waldo Emerson, the American poet and philosopher known for his rejection of a personal God, who once said that consistency is the hobgoblin of little minds.

The pros and cons of the Patriot Act can leave Red Letter Christians perplexed, but we must think through its implications in faithfulness to our calling. Again, it is worth remembering Philippians 2:12, which reminds us to work out our salvation daily, with fear and trembling. Regardless how we come out on this matter, it is imperative that those running for office be asked whether the Patriot Act should stand, be abolished or be changed. And if their answer is that it should be modified, he or she should spell out the specific changes he or she hopes to make.

God's Kingdom and the Political Landscape

There are other political issues that merit attention but cannot be explored here with the care and depth they deserve. For instance, the question of whether or not the government should sponsor—or even allow—stem cell research is becoming more and more prominent in political discussions. Some Christians forcefully argue that the human embryo should be treated as a sacred creation of God, worthy of spiritual dignity. Others claim that it is wrong to waste embryos that will be destroyed anyway, when they might be used to cure illnesses such as Parkinson's and Alzheimer's disease, or to restore para- and quadriplegics to the full use of their bodies. Because the political landscape changes so rapidly, this may become a dominant issue in upcoming elections while Christian ethicists argue the pros and cons.

On the other hand, by the time you read this book, some of the issues dealt with here will have become passé. Hopefully, the ways I have reflected on politics from my personal understanding of Scripture will encourage you to develop your own Christian perspective on the pressing political issues of the day.

Red Letter Christians are likely to have differences of opinion with other deeply committed Christians—and even with each other. In the give-and-take between Christians with differing political priorities, there have to be some ground rules if we are to live as citizens of God's Kingdom even as we seek to expand it. While I have been challenged by my students to rethink my positions on social issues, I have, in turn, challenged them to consider carefully how they engage those with differing points of view.

First, I tell them, we must avoid name-calling or demonizing those who disagree with us. There is something terribly wrong when Christians with liberal political ideas call those on the Religious Right "fascists," and something equally wrong when the retort of political conservatives is to call those who lean Left "communists." Such name-calling is condemned by Jesus Himself (see Matt. 5:22).

Second, when taking a stand on a political issue, we must entertain the possibility that we might be wrong. Looking back over the years, I can recall many instances when I was so sure of myself on a certain issue, only to eventually realize I was very, very wide of the mark. Authentic dialogue on political issues cannot take place unless those on each side entertain the possibility that there may be truth in the opposing point of view. If we don't approach dialogue with this kind of humility, we only end up shouting at each other until we run out of energy, passion and time.

I know two women who were on opposite sides of the abortion issue. One worked with Planned Parenthood, a pro-choice organization, and the other worked with a Roman Catholic crisis pregnancy center. But instead of calling each other names, they were humble enough to talk to and learn from each other. The pro-choice woman came to a deeper appreciation of the sacredness of all life, and the pro-life woman came to an understanding of how economic factors often drive women to seek abortions, and how pregnancies resulting from rape or incest were viewed by her pro-choice friend.

Third, we must try to find common ground—or, as my friend Jim Wallis says, "higher ground." In spite of our differences, there are many concerns Christians hold in common. Many Red Letter Christians have joined Wallis's Call to Renewal movement, which brings together Christians from across the political spectrum to work together to "Make Poverty History!" Call to Renewal is an example of the good that can be accomplished when Christians walk forward together on higher ground.

Most Christians will affirm that politics are far too serious to be left in the hands of politicians. We should be agreed that God holds all of us responsible for making decisions that determine our national and global destiny. In the end, we will all be judged by our answers to two questions: *What have you decided about Me and the way of salvation I have provided?* and *What have you done to allow My Kingdom to come on earth, even as it is in heaven?*

Only where God's Kingdom has come to earth can there be justice for the poor and oppressed—for any of us.

ENDNOTES

Chapter 1: Who Are Red Letter Christians?

1. "Quality of Life: Hunger," Global Energy Network Institute, 7/12/07. http://www.geni.org/globalenergy/issues/global/qualityoflife/hunger/index.shtml (accessed September 2007). See also "Hunger Facts," Compassion International. http://www.compassion.com/child-advocacy/find-your-voice/quick-facts/hunger-quick-facts.htm (accessed September 2007).
2. Anup Shah, "U.S. and Foreign Aid Assistance," Global Issues, 4/8/07. http://www.globalissues.org/TradeRelated/Debt/USAid.asp (accessed September 2007).
3. "U.S. and World Population Clocks," U.S. Census Bureau, 9/11/07. http://www.census.gov/main/www/popclock.html (accessed September 2007).
4. Ben Somberg, "The World's Most Generous Misers," FAIR, 10/05. http://www.fair.org/index.php?page=2676 (accessed September 2007).
5. "Camden City 2003," CAMConnect, 3/03. http://www.camconnect.org/fact/documents/camden_city.pdf (accessed September 2007).
6. CAMConnect, Camden Facts, Demographics 2006. http://www.camconnect.org/documents/camden_facts_2006.pdf (accessed October 2007).
7. Medline Plus, hospitals with emergency services within 25 miles of Camden, NJ. http://apps.nlm.nih.gov/medlineplus/directories/index.cfm?action=results&type=hosp&lang=us&criteria=byCity&fromSearch=true&stateSelected=NJ&citySelected=Camden&specialty=&service=EMERH (accessed October 2007).
8. "2003 Uniform Crime Report," New Jersey State Police, 2003. http://www.state.nj.us/lps/njsp/info/ucr2003/index.html (accessed September 2007).
9. Ibid.
10. Ibid.
11. Iver Petersen "A Mayor's Fateful Journey from Camden's Streets to Jail; Caught Up in the City's Tangle of Corruption," *The New York Times,* January 3, 2001. http://query.nytimes.com/gst/fullpage.html?res=9B00EFDB103BF930A35752C0A9679C8B63 (accessed September 2007).
12. Tom Knoche, *Common Sense for Camden: Taking Back Our City* (Camden, N.J., 2005) pp. 25-27.
13. Ibid., p. 6.
14. Ibid., p. 7.
15. "The Number of Uninsured Americans Is at an All-Time High," Center on Budget and Policy Priorities, 8/29/06. http://www.cbpp.org/8-29-06health.htm (accessed September 2007).
16. Jeanne Sahadi, "CEO Pay: 364 Time More Than Workers," CNN Money, 8/29/07. http://money.cnn.com/2007/08/28/news/economy/ceo_pay_workers/index.htm (accessed September 2007). See also Jeanne Sahadi, "CEO Paycheck: $42,000 a day," CNN Money, 6/21/2006. http://money.cnn.com/2006/06/21/news/companies/ceo_pay_epi/index.htm?section=money_topstories (accessed September 2007).
17. Personal interview with President Bill Clinton in Chappaqua, NY.
18. "Number in Poverty and Poverty Rate: 1959 to 2005," U.S. Census Bureau. http://www.census.gov/hhes/www/poverty/poverty05/graphs05.html (accessed September 2007).
19. Stephanie Armour, "Homelessness Grows as More Live Check-to-Check," *USA Today*, 8/12/03. http://www.usatoday.com/money/economy/2003-08-11-homeless_x.htm (accessed September 2007).
20. "Background and Statistics," National Coalition for Homeless Veterans. http://www.nchv.org/background.cfm (accessed September 2007).
21. NCH Fact Sheet #2, "How Many People Experience Homelessness?" National Coalition for the Homeless, August 2007. Available for download at http://www.nationalhomeless.org/publications/facts.html (accessed September 2007).

22. "Deforestation Exacerbates Haiti Floods," *USA Today*, 9/23/2004. http://www.usatoday.com/weather/hurricane/2004-09-23-haiti-deforest_x.htm (accessed September 2007).
23. "The Relationship Between Drought and Famine," Food and Agriculture Organization of the United Nations. http://www.unu.edu/unupress/unupbooks/uu22we/uu22we0b.htm (accessed September 2007).

Chapter 2: A Biblical Approach to Politics

1. Hendrik Berkhof, *Christ and the Powers* (Scottdale, PA: Herald Press, 1977), pp. 18-26.
2. Max Weber, *The Theory of Social and Economic Organization*, translated by A. M. Henderson and Talcott Parsons (New York: The Free Press, 1965), p. 152.
3. Isaac Watts, "When I Survey the Wondrous Cross" (1707), music by Lowell Mason (1824).

Chapter 3: The Environment

1. "The Ecological Cost of Meat," Animal Connection of Texas. http://www.animalconnectiontx.org/home/ecological.htm (accessed September 2007).
2. Roger A. Pielke, Sr. and Christopher A. Davey, "Microclimate Exposures of Surface-based Weather Stations–Implications for the Assessment of Long-term Temperature Trends," *Bulletin of the American Meteorological Society*, 2005, 86(4), pp. 497–504.
3. Carl Wunsch, "Swindled: Carl Wunsch Responds," RealClimate, March 12, 2007. http://www.realclimate.org/index.php/archives/2007/03/swindled-carl-wunsch-responds/#more-417 (accessed October 2007).
4. Mendelson's testimony to the U.S. Senate quoted by Christopher C. Horner, "Global Warming: A Guide to the Hype," Insider Online, Spring 2007. http://www.insideronline.org/archives/2007/spring/chap1.pdf (accessed October 2007).
5. Bill Blakemore, "The Psychology of Global Warming: Alarm-ist Versus Alarm-ing," ABC News, December 8, 2005. http://abcnews.go.com/Technology/GlobalWarming/story?id=1387081 (accessed October 2007).
6. Mark Knox, "Global Warming Debate Generates Resolution Heat," *The Baptist Standard*, 6/14/07. http://www.baptiststandard.com/postnuke/index.php?module=htmlpages&func=display&pid=6466 (accessed August 2007). See also Bob Allen, "Southern Baptists Reject Scientific Consensus About Global Warming," EthicsDaily.com, 6/14/07. http://www.ethicsdaily.com/article_detail.cfm?AID=9058 (accessed September 2007).
7. "UN Climate Change Impact Report: Poor Will Suffer Most," Environment News Service, April 7, 2006. http://www.ens-newswire.com/ens/apr2007/2007-04-06-01.asp (accessed August 2007).
8. "Wind Energy in Germany," Germany WindEnergy Association (BWE), www.wind-energie.de/en. http://www.wind-energie.de/en/wind-energy-in-germany/ (accessed August 2007).
9. "What Is the Kyoto Treaty?" BBC News, September 23, 2003. http://news.bbc.co.uk/1/hi/world/europe/2233897.stm (accessed October 2007).
10. "Impacts of the Kyoto Protocol on U.S. Energy Markets and Economic Activity," Energy Information Administration. http://www.eia.doe.gov/oiaf/kyoto/kyotorpt.html (accessed October 2007).
11. "China's Challenge to the Kyoto Protocol," China Environmental News Digest, December 12, 2006. http://china-environmental-news.blogspot.com/2006/12/chinas-challenge-to-kyoto-protocol.html (accessed October 2007).
12. "G8 Leaders Strike Deal to Cut Emissions in Half by 2050," CBC News, June 7, 2007. http://www.cbc.ca/world/story/2007/06/07/g8-climatechange.html?ref=rss (accessed October 2007).
13. "Blair and Bush Say Differences Remain Over Global Warming," *International Herald Tribune*, July 7, 2005. http://www.iht.com/articles/2005/07/07/europe/web.0707blair.php (accessed October 2007).
14. A. J. Surrey and A. J. Browley, "Energy Resources" in H. S. D. Cole, Christopher Freeman, Marei Jahoda, K. L. R. Pavitt (editors), *Models of Doom* (New York: Universe Books, 1978), pp. 90-101.

15. Tony Campolo and Gordon Aeschliman, *50 Ways You Can Help Save the Planet* (Downers Grove, IL: InterVarsity Press, 1992), pp. 63-64.
16. E. O. Wilson, *The Creation*, (London: W. W. Norton and Company, Inc., 2006), p. 31.
17. Donella H. Meadows, Dennis Meadows, Jorgeu Renders and William W. Behrens III, *The Limits to Growth* (New York: Universe Books, 1972), pp. 78-80.
18. Ibid. See also Walter Schneir, "The Atom's Poisonous Garbage," *The Reporter*, 1960.
19. Lawrence Hajna, "U.S. Judge to Rule If Cement Plant Can Operate," *Courier-Post*, 3/24/01.
20. "Chernobyl: Assessment of Radiological and Health Impact," Nuclear Energy Agency, 2002. http://www.nea.fr/html/rp/chernobyl/c05.html (accessed September 2007)
21. "Disposal of Nuclear Waste," *The African Potato*. http://theafricanpotato.110mb.com/nuclear/waste/nuclearwaste.html (accessed September 2007). See also Walter Schneir, "The Atom's Poisonous Garbage," *The Reporter*, 1960.

Chapter 4: The War

1. "Just War Theory: The *Jus Ad Bellum* Convention," The Internet Encyclopedia of Philosophy, www.iep.utm.edu. http://www.iep.utm.edu/j/justwar.htm#H2 (accessed August 2007).
2. Bill Moyers and Kathleen Hughes, *Buying the War*, PBS, originally broadcast on April 25, 2007. http://www.pbs.org/moyers/journal/btw/transcript1.html (accessed August 2007).
3. Erin O'Brien, "Democracy and Homeland Security: Strategies, Controversies and Impact," The Kent State University Press. http://upress.kent.edu/ammar/12%20Obrien.htm (accessed September 2007). See also Jeffrey M. Jones, "Nearly Nine in Ten Americans Believe bin Laden Associates in United States," 9/17/02. http://www.galluppoll.com/content/?ci=6829&pg=1 (accessed September 2007); Steven Kull, Clay Ramsay, Stefan Subias and Evan Lewis, "US Public Beliefs on Iraq and the Presidential Election," The PIPA/Knowledge Networks Poll, 4/22/04. http://www.pipa.org/OnlineReports/Iraq/IraqBeliefs_Apr04/IraqBeliefs%20Apr04%20quaire.pdf (accessed September 2007).
4. "Straw Withdraws 45 Minutes Claim," BBC News, 10/12/04. http://news.bbc.co.uk/1/hi/uk_politics/3736086.stm (accessed September 2007).
5. "Public Struggles with Possible War in Iraq," The Pew Research Center, 01/30/03. http://people-press.org/commentary/display.php3?AnalysisID=60 (accessed September 2007).
6. Mark Leibovich, "George Tenet's 'Slam-Dunk' Into the History Books," *The Washington Post*, 6/4/04. http://www.washingtonpost.com/ac2/wp-dyn/A14030-2004Jun3 (accessed September 2007).
7. "Taking Measure of Iraq's Progress Towards Democracy," U.S. Senate Republican Policy Committee, 6/22/04. http://rpc.senate.gov/_files/June2204IraqDF.pdf (accessed September 2007).
8. "Press Briefing Scott McClellan," The White House, 6/27/05. http://www.whitehouse.gov/news/releases/2005/06/print/20050627-3.html (accessed September 2007).
9. Dana Priest, "Iraq New Terror Breeding Ground," *The Washington Post*, 1/14/05. http://www.washingtonpost.com/wp-dyn/articles/A7460-2005Jan13.html (accessed September 2007).
10. "Beyond Red vs. Blue: Republicans Divided About Role of Government, Democrats by Social and Personal Values—Part 6: Issues and Shifting Coalitions," Pew Research Center for the People and the Press, 5/10/05. http://people-press.org/reports/print.php3?PageID=948 (accessed September 2007).
11. The opinion was expressed by fellow guests when I appeared on the George Stephanopoulus television show *This Week* on November 28, 2004. The guests included Gary Bauer, George Weigel and Floyd Flake. See also Gilbert Burnham, Riyadh Lafta, Shannon Doocy and Les Roberts, "Mortality After the 2003 Invasion of Iraq: A Cross-Sectional Cluster Sample Survey," The Lancet.com, 10/11/06. http://66.102.1.104/scholar?hl=en&lr=&q=cache:7R_yCKvhbOEJ:engforit.tripod.com/library/New%2520Library/mortalityiraq.pdf+ (accessed September of 2007).
12. Dan Murphy, "Iraqis Thirst for Water and Power," *The Christian Science Monitor*, 08/11/05. http://www.csmonitor.com/2005/0811/p01s03-woiq.html (accessed September 2007).

13. Doug Struck, "Professionals Fleeing Iraq as Violence, Threats Persist," *The Washington Post*, 01/23/06. http://www.washingtonpost.com/wp-dyn/content/article/2006/01/22/AR20060 12201112.html (accessed September 2007).
14. Walter Wykes, "A Prayer for the People of Iraq," Ezine Articles. http://ezinearticles.com/? A-Prayer-for-the-People-of-iraq&id=711421 (accessed September 2007).
15. "More Iraq Vets Seek Mental Health Care," CBS News, 3/1/06. http://www.cbsnews.com/ stories/2006/03/01/iraq/main1357296.shtml (accessed September 2007). See also "Akaka Introduces Bill to Extend Health Care for Returning Troops," U.S. Senator of Hawaii: Press Releases, 01/24/07. http://akaka.senate.gov/public/index.cfm?FuseAction=PressReleases.Home& month=1&year=2007&release_id=1506 (accessed September 2007).
16. Travis Sharp, "The Bucks Never Stop: Iraq and Afghanistan War Costs Continue to Soar," Center for Arms Control and Non-Proliferation. http://armscontrolcenter.org/policy/secu rityspending/articles/bucks_never_stop/ (accessed September 2007).
17. "Major Foreign Holders of Treasury Securities," U.S. Department of Treasury. http://www.us treas.gov/tic/mfh.txt (accessed September 2007). See also James Surowiecki, "In Yuan We Trust," *The New Yorker*, 4/18/05. http://www.newyorker.com/archive/2005/04/18/050418 ta_talk_surowiecki (accessed September 2007); "Experts Warn that Heavy Debt Threatens American Economy," *USA Today*. http://www.usatoday.com/money/economy/2005-08-27-growing-debt_x.htm (accessed September 2007); William Schneider, "Re-evaluating U.S. Debt," The Atlantic.com, 10/25/05. http://www.theatlantic.com/doc/prem/200510u/nj_ schneider_2005-10-25 (accessed September 2007); Paul B. Farrell, "China Loves Blackstone's 'American Dream'," Market Watch, 5/28/2007. http://www.marketwatch.com/news/story/ chinas-new-ownership-society---/story.aspx?guid=%7B4A3ECBE2%2DE799% 2D4DAE%2D9FF2%2DCF591A394698%7D (accessed September 2007); "Who Wants to be a Trillionaire?" *The Economist*, 10/26/06. http://www.economist.com/finance/displaystory.cfm? story_id=8083036 (accessed September 2007).
18. Letters from George Verwer, founder and past president of Operation Mobilisation, a missionary organization that has missionaries in several Muslim nations.
19. "Christians in Iraq Face Persecution, Need Protection, U.S. Bishops State," Catholic Online, 10/31/06. http://www.catholic.org/national/national_story.php?id=21815 (accessed September 2007).
20. "June 2007 10/40 Window Prayer Focus: The Year of Prayer for North Korea and Far East Nations," Window International Network. http://www.win1040.com/WINEmailNews/WINE mailNewsJune2007.pdf (accessed September 2007).
21. *Christianity Today*, January 2007, p. 22.
22. Story told to author by Millard Fuller, founder of the Habitat for Humanity, who received the story from Clarence Jordon of Koinonia Farms, who was present at this event.
23. James Martone, "Iraq Condemns Embargo on 9th Anniversary of Sanctions," CNN, 8/6/99. http://www.cnn.com/WORLD/meast/9908/06/iraq.sanctions/ (accessed September 2007).
24. "New Poll: 71 Percent of Iraqis Want U.S. Forces to Withdraw Within a Year," Think Progress, 9/27/06. http://thinkprogress.org/2006/09/27/iraqis-poll/ (accessed September 2007).
25. "British Ex-Army Chief Criticizes U.S. Over Iraq," Yahoo News, 9/1/07. http://news.yahoo.com /s/nm/20070901/wl_nm/britain_iraq_jackson_dc (accessed September 2007).
26. Raed Jarrar and Joshua Holland, "Majority of Iraqi Lawmakers Now Reject Occupation," AlterNet, 5/7/07. http://www.alternet.org/waroniraq/51624 (accessed September 2007).
27. To view the proposal in its entirety, visit http://www.tikkun.org/iraqpeace.

Chapter 5: Palestine

1. General Assembly, "A/RES/181 (II) (A+B) of 29 November 1947," United Nations, 11/29/47. http://domino.un.org/unispal.nsf/dbe273e151ef674d85256cbe0070e688/7f0af2bd897689 b785256c330061d253!OpenDocument (accessed September 2007).
2. Jimmy Carter, *Palestine: Peace Not Apartheid* (New York: Simon and Schuster, 2006), p. 58.

3. Elias Chacour, *Blood Brothers* (Grand Rapids, MI: Chosen Books, 2003), chapter 3. This chapter gives an overview of the consequences of the displacement of Palestinians. See also Michael Lerner, *Healing Israel/Palestine: A Path to Peace and Reconciliation* (Berkley, CA: North Atlantic Books, 2003), pp. 61-71.
4. Carter, *Palestine: Peace Not Apartheid*, p. 58.
5. Ibid., p. 132.
6. Security Council, "S/RES/242 (1967 of 22 November 1967)," United Nations, 11/22/67. http://domino.un.org/unispal.nsf/9fb163c870bb1d6785256cef0073c89f/7d35e1f729df491c85256ee700686136!OpenDocument (accessed September 2007).
7. Security Council, "S/RES/338 (1973) of 22 October 1973," United Nations, 10/22/73. http://domino.un.org/unispal.nsf/dcb71e2bf9f2dca585256cef0073ed5d/7fb7c26fcbe80a31852560c50065f878!OpenDocument (accessed September 2007).
8. Carter, *Palestine: Peace Not Apartheid*, pp. 174, 189.
9. "Israel and the Occupied Territories: The Place of the Fence/Wall in International Law," Amnesty International, 2/19/04. http://web.amnesty.org/library/Index/ENGMDE150162004 (accessed September 2007).
10. Ibid.
11. Ibid.
12. Carter, *Palestine: Peace Not Apartheid*, p. 211.
13. "Statement Attributable to the Spokesman for the Secretary-General on the 'Geneva Accord,'" Secretary-General Office of the Spokesperson, 11/5/03. http://www.un.org/apps/sg/sgstats.asp?nid=610 (accessed September 2007).
14. Carter, *Palestine: Peace Not Apartheid*, pp. 157-162.
15. "Pat Robertson Apologizes to Israel," CBS News, 1/12/06. http://www.cbsnews.com/stories/2006/01/12/world/main1206289.shtml (accessed September 2007).
16. Carter, *Palestine: Peace Not Apartheid*, p. 209. Cites a poll taken by the *International Herald Tribune* in October 2003.
17. From a personal conversation with Senator Paul Simon of Illinois, 8/30/02, Renaissance Conference at Beaver Creek, CO.
18. Betty Jane Bailey and J. Martin Bailey, *Who Are the Christians in the Middle East?* (Grand Rapids, MI: Wm. B. Eerdmans, 2003), pp. 152-158.
19. Donald E. Wagner, *Dying in the Land of Promise* (London: Melisende, 2001), pp. 208-209.

Chapter 6: The AIDS Pandemic

1. "Number with HIV 'At Highest Yet'," BBC News, 10/21/05. http://news.bbc.co.uk/1/hi/health/4450872.stm (accessed September 2007).
2. "Children, HIV and AIDS," Avert, 8/17/07. http://www.avert.org/children.htm (accessed September 2007).
3. The DATA Report 2007, p. 65.
4. "Right Wing Watch: Justice Sunday III Speaker Backgrounder," People for the American Way. http://www.pfaw.org/pfaw/general/default.aspx?oid=20267 (accessed September 2007).
5. Bono, quoted by Andy Argyrakis, "Backstage with Bono," *Christianity Today*, 12/09/02. http://www.christianitytoday.com/music/interviews/bono-1202.html (accessed August 2007).
6. John Donnelly, "With AIDS Funding Proposal, Bush Looks to His Legacy," *The Boston Globe*, 5/31/07. http:// www.boston.com/news/world/articles/2007/05/31/with_aids_funding_proposal_bush_looks_to_his_legacy/ (accessed September 2007).
7. Barbara Hagenbaugh, "Greenspan Takes Center Stage in 'Age of Turbulence'," *USA Today*, 9/17/07, p. 2B.
8. "The Context: HIV," Catholic Agency for Overseas Development. http://www.cafod.org.uk/news_and_events/media_centre/hiv/the_context (accessed September 2007).

9. Laurie B. Sylla, "Microbicides: Worthy of More Attention," Yale University Center for Interdisciplinary Research on Aids, 3/31/01. http://cira.med.yale.edu/law_policy_ethics/policy updatevol3iss2.pdf (accessed September 2007).
10. "Mbeki Accuses CIA over AIDS," BBC News, 10/6/00. http://news.bbc.co.uk/2/hi/africa/959579.stm (accessed September 2007). See also Richard Knox, "Origin of AIDS Linked to Colonial Practices in Africa," NPR. http://www.npr.org/templates/story/story.php?storyId=5450391 (accessed September 2007).
11. Michael Kranish, "Religious Right Wields Clout," *The Boston Globe*, 10/9/06. http://www.boston.com/news/nation/articles/2006/10/09/religious_right_wields_clout/?page=3 (accessed September 2007).
12. "Ugandan Condom Crisis," Health Global Access Project, 08/05. http://www.healthgap.org/press_releases/05/0805_CHANGE_HGAP_FS_Uganda_condoms.pdf (accessed September 2007).
13. The CEO who told me this story wished to remain anonymous.
14. This information was provided by Michael Cassidy of African Enterprise Evangelistic Association at the SACLA conference in Pretoria, South Africa, July 10, 2003.

Chapter 7: Gay Rights

1. John F. Harris, "Victory Bears Out Emphasis on Values," *The Washington Post*, 10/4/04. http://www.washingtonpost.com/ac2/wp-dyn/A23671-2004Nov3?language=printer (accessed September 2007); Ben Adler, "Gay Marriage Policy No Linchpin for GOP," CBS News, 10/14/06. http://www.cbsnews.com/stories/2006/11/14/opinion/printable2180046.shtml (accessed September 2007); Rachel Clarke, "Drawing Up Blueprints for Bush Victory," BBC News, 10/6/04. http://news.bbc.co.uk/2/hi/americas/3987237.stm (accessed September 2007).
2. Ibid.
3. David G. Myers, "Accepting What Cannot Be Changed," in Walter Wink, *Homosexuality and Christian Faith* (Minneapolis, MN: Augsburg Fortress Press, 1999), pp. 68-69.
4. William Stacy Johnson, *A Time to Embrace* (Grand Rapids, MI: Wm. B. Eerdmans, 2006), pp. 25-28.
5. In discussions with William Kephart and James H. S. Bossard, my colleagues at the University of Pennsylvania, there was agreement that female homosexuality was more social-psychological than with males, but there is no "hard" empirical evidence to support this.
6. Johnson, *A Time to Embrace*, pp. 25-28.
7. Myers, "Accepting What Cannot Be Changed," in Walter Wink, *Homosexuality and Christian Faith*, pp. 68-69.
8. *The eCable*, Fall 2007, Evangelicals Concerned, Inc., p. 11.
9. The U.S. Episcopal Church (ECUSA) has supported the ordination of a gay Bishop and has voted to approve gay marriages. The United Church of Christ (UCC) has also approved gay marriages. The Evangelical Lutheran Church of America (ELCA) has voted to not penalize gay clergy who are in "marital" relationships with a partner of the same sex.
10. The Pew Research Center for the People and the Press, "Republicans Unified, Democrats Split on Gay Marriage: Religious Beliefs Underpin Opposition to Homosexuality," November 18, 2003. http://pewforum.org/publications/surveys/religion-homosexuality.pdf (accessed September 2007).
11. The Pew Research Center for The People and the Press, "Only 34% Favor South Dakota Abortion Ban, Less Opposition to Gay Marriage, Adoption and Military Service," March 22, 2006. http://people-press.org/reports/pdf/273.pdf (accessed September 2007).
12. Dennis Cauchon, "Civil Unions Gain Support," *USA Today*, March 9, 2004. http://www.usatoday.com/news/nation/2004-03-09-gaymarriage-usat_x.htm (accessed September 2007).
13. U.S. General Accounting Office, *Defense of Marriage Act*, GAO/OGC-97-16 (Washington, DC: January 31, 1997). http://www.gao.gov/archive/1997/og97016.pdf (accessed September 2007). After passage of the Defense of Marriage Act of 1996, Congress requested that the Government Accountability Office (GAO) "identify federal laws in which benefits, rights, and privi-

leges are contingent on marital status." The GAO identified 13 categories and 1,049 federal laws involving marital status. In 2004, the list was updated by the GAO: "Consequently, as of December 31, 2003, our re-search identified a total of 1,138 federal statutory provisions classified to the United States Code in which marital status is a factor in determining or receiving benefits, rights, and privileges." http://www.gao.gov/new.items/d04353r.pdf (accessed September 2007).

14. According to the GAO, in a report released February 24, 2005, an estimated 9,500 services members were dismissed between 1994 and 2003 for homosexual conduct. U.S. Government Accountability Office, "Military Personnel: Financial Costs and Loss of Critical Skills Due to DOD's Homosexual Conduct Policy Cannot Be Completely Estimated," February 24, 2005. http://www.gao.gov/htext/ d05299.html (accessed September 2007).
15. Gen. John M. Shalikashvili, "Second Thoughts on Gays in the Military," *The New York Times*, January 2, 2007. http://www.nytimes.com/2007/01/02/opinion/02shalikashvili.html?ex=1325394000&en=171a9a25f632cbde&ei=5088&partner=rssnyt&emc=rss (accessed August 2007).
16. "Births, Marriages, Divorces, and Deaths: Provisional Data for 2005," National Vital Statistics Reports, Volume 54, Number 20, July 21, 2006. http://www.cdc.gov/nchs/data/nvsr/nvsr54/nvsr54_20.pdf (accessed September 2007).
17. Martin O'Connell and Gretchen Gooding, "Editing Unmarried Couples in Census Bureau Data," U.S. Bureau of the Census, July 2007. http://www.census.gov/population/www/documentation/twps07/twps07.html (accessed September 2007).
18. Transcript of President's Remarks, The White House, Office of Press Secretary, President Defends Sanctity of Marriage, November 18, 2003. http://www.whitehouse.gov/news/releases/2003/11/20031118-4.html (accessed September 2007). See also Transcript of President's Radio Address, July 10, 2004. http://www.whitehouse.gov/news/releases/2004/07/20040710.html (accessed September 2007).
19. Simon Barrow and Jonathan Bartley, "What Future for Marriage?" *Ekklesia*, revised July, 2006. http://www.ekklesia.co.uk/research/papers/abolishmarriage (accessed September 2007).
20. From informal professional discussions with colleagues when speaking at universities and colleges across the country.
21. Howard Witt, "Anti-hate law shifts to debate on gays," *Chicago Tribune* web edition, August 13, 2007. http://www.chicagotribune.com/news/nationworld/chi-hate_newaug13,1,2186019.story?page=1&ctrack=1&cset=true (accessed September 2007).
22. The House of Representatives, Committee of the Judiciary, April 25, 2007, transcripts, p. 206, lines 4854-4871. http://judiciary.house.gov/Media/PDFS/Transcripts/transcript070425.pdf (accessed September 2007).
23. Tommy Thompson, California Republican Debate Transcript, MSNBC, May 4, 2007. http://www.msnbc.msn.com/id/18478985/ (accessed September 2007).
24. "Questions and Answers: The Local Law Enforcement Hate Crimes Prevention Act," Human Rights Campaign, January 17, 2007, p. 2. http://www.matthewshepard.org/site/DocServer/HRC-LLEHCPA-FAQ1-17-07.pdf?docID=463 (accessed September 2007).
25. Chris Bull, *Perfect Enemies: The Battle Between the Religious Right and the Gay Movement* (Lanham, MD: Madison Books, updated edition, 2001).

Chapter 8: Gun Control

1. Erich Pratt, "2001: The Year in Review: GOA Members Help Put Guns Back Onto Planes," Gun Owners of America, 12/21/01. http://www.gunowners.org/news/nws0112.htm (accessed September 2007).
2. Peter Brown, "Vtech Shows Gun Control Has Lost Its Political Luster," Real Clear Politics, 4/23/07. http://www.realclearpolitics.com/articles/2007/04/vtech_shows_gun_control_has_lo.html (accessed September 2007).

3. "Second Amendment Survey," Second Amendment Foundation. http://www.saf.org/Law Reviews/Pierce1.html (accessed September 2007).
4. Ibid.
5. Marshall Loeb, "Americans Can," *TIME* magazine, 7/10/72. http://www.time.com/time/magazine/article/0,9171,910350-1,00.html (accessed September 2007).
6. "Guns, Gun Ownership, & RTC at All-Time Highs, Less 'Gun Control,' and Violent Crime at 30-Year Low," NRA Institute for Legislative Action. http://www.nraila.org/Issues/FactSheets/Read.aspx?ID=126 (accessed September 2007).
7. "Questions and Answers: Gun Show Loophole Closing and Gun Law Enforcement Bill," Senator Joe Lieberman: News Release, 5/15/01. http://lieberman.senate.gov/newsroom/release.cfm?id=208581 (accessed September 2007).
8. John Rosenthal, "Too Little, Too Late Policy-Making for Gun Control," The Huffington Post, 5/1/07. http://www.huffingtonpost.com/john-rosenthal/too-little-too-late-poli_b_47421.html (accessed September 2007).
9. Jake Tapper and Avery Miller, "'Mentally Ill' but Still Able to Buy a Gun," ABC News, April 19, 2007. http://abcnews.go.com/WNT/VATech/story?id=3059185&page=1 (accessed October 2007).
10. Marian Wright Edelman, "Protect Children, Not Guns," Children's Defense Fund, 2007. http://www.childrensdefense.org/site/News2?id=8569&page=NewsArticle (accessed October 2007).
11. Courtney Humphries, "Child Firearm Deaths Tied to Gun Availability," *Focus,* Harvard School of Public Health, March 8, 2002. http://focus.hms.harvard.edu/2002/March8_2002/injury_control.html (accessed October 2007).
12. Bob Herbert, "An American Addiction," *International Herald Tribune*, April 26, 2007.
13. Jenna Oskowitz, "State Homocide Rate in '06 Fell, but Not Here," *Philly News,* September 22, 2007. http://www.philly.com/dailynews/local/20070922_State_homicide_rate_in_06_fell_but_not_here.html (accessed October 2007).

Chapter 9: Education

1. "Comparative School District Data," Good Schools Pennsylvania, 2006. http://www.goodschoolspa.org/pdf/2005-06%20County%20Sheets.pdf (accessed September 2007).
2. Remark by David W. Hornbeck, Philadelphia Superintendent of Schools, before the General Assembly of the National Council of Churches, November 11, 1998.
3. Abby Goodnough, "Camden Asks New Jersey to Take Over School System," *The New York Times,* March 26, 1998. http://query.nytimes.com/gst/fullpage.html?res=9905E7D71F38F935A15750C0A96E958260&sec=&spon=&pagewanted=print (accessed October 2007).
4. Wayne Flynt, "Rural Poverty in America," National Forum, Summer 1996. http://findarticles.com/p/articles/mi_qa3651/is_199607/ai_n8740870 (accessed September 2007).
5. Paul E. Peterson, Jay P. Greene and Chad Noyes, "School Choice in Milwaukee," *The Public Interest*, Fall 1996.
6. Barbara A. Grant, press release from the School District of Philadelphia, "Philadelphia Students Out-Perform Voucher/Edison Students," 5/28/99.
7. Most commonly, Engle v. Vitale (1962), Abington School District v. Schempp (1963) and Lemon v. Kurtzman (1971).
8. For a summary of the views of Horace Mann, see Lawrence A. Cremin (editor), *The Republic and the School: Horace Mann on the Education of Free Man* (New York: Teachers College Press, 1957).
9. Melanie Burney and Frank Kummer, "Roots of Cheating in Camden Run Deep," *Philadelphia Inquirer*, 12/17/06. http://www.mywire.com/pubs/PhiladelphiaInquirer/2006/12/17/2315094?&pbl=17 (accessed September 2007). See also Ford Fessenden, "Schools Under Scrutiny Over Cheating," *The New York Times*, 9/9/07. http://www.nytimes.com/2007/09/09/nyregion/nyregionspecial2/09Rcheating.html?_r=1&oref=slogin (accessed September 2007).
10. Greg Toppo, "Study: No Child Left Behind Seems to Be Working," *USA Today*. http:// www.usatoday.com/news/education/2007-06-05-nclb-report_n.htm (accessed September 2007).

Chapter 10: Abortion

1. Joseph Cardinal Bernardin, "A Consistent Ethic of Life: Continuing the Dialogue," a lecture delivered at St. Louis University's William Wade Lecture Series on March 11, 1984. http://www.priestsforlife.org/magisterium/bernardinwade.html (accessed August 2007).
2. Joerg Dreweke and Rebecca Wind, "Expanding Access to Contraception Through Medicaid Could Prevent Nearly 500,000 Unwanted Pregnancies, Save $1.5 Billion," Guttmacher Institute, 8/16/06. http://guttmacher.org/media/nr/2006/08/16/index.html (accessed September 2007).
3. Ibid. See also Jennifer J. Frost, Adam Sonfield and Rachael Benson Gold, "Estimating the Impact of Expanding Medicaid Eligibility for Family Planning Services," Occasional Report of the Guttmacher Institute, 2006, No. 28, pp. 23-25.
4. Holly Sklar and Rev. James A. Forbes Jr., "A Just Minimum Wage: Good for Workers, Business and Our Future," Let Justice Roll, 2005. http://www.letjusticeroll.org/pdfs/AJustMinimumWage.pdf (accessed September 2007).
5. Dreweke and Wind, "Expanding Access to Contraception Through Medicaid Could Prevent Nearly 500,000 Unwanted Pregnancies, Save $1.5 Billion."
6. For more information, visit the "95-10" information page at the Democrats for Life website. http://www.democratsforlife.org/index.php?option=com_content&task=view&id=48&Itemid=45 (accessed August 2007).
7. "United States Abortion Statistics: Reported abortions in the United States by year, 1973-2005," ©Minnesota Citizens Concerned for Life. http://www.mccl.org/abortion_statistics.htm (accessed August 2007).
8. "Chronological Archives of Major Issues Are Now on Layman Online," *The Layman* online, 1/10/07. http://www.layman.org/layman/Archive1/issues%20by%20category.htm (accessed September 2007).
9. House of Representatives Press Release, "Davis Introduces Comprehensive Proposal to Reduce Abortions in America," September 20, 2006. http://www.house.gov/lincolndavis/releaseseptember202006.htm (accessed August 2007).
10. Dreweke and Wind, "Expanding Access to Contraception Through Medicaid Could Prevent Nearly 500,000 Unwanted Pregnancies, Save $1.5 Billion."

Chapter 11: Immigration

1. Pew Hispanic Center, "Modes of Entry for the Illegal Immigrant Population," May 22, 2006. http://pewhispanic.org/files/factsheets/19.pdf (accessed August 2007).
2. Juliana Barbassa, "Despite Controversy, Illegal Immigrants File Taxes More than Ever," *North County Times*, 4/12/07. http://www.nctimes.com/articles/2007/04/13/news/state/13_17_204_12_07.txt (accessed September 2007). See also Eduardo Porter, "Illegal Immigrants Are Bolstering Social Security with Billions," *The New York Times*, 4/5/05. http://www.nytimes.com/2005/04/05/business/05immigration.html?_r=1&oref=slogin (accessed September 2007).
3. Ibid.
4. According to several Social Security representatives.
5. From personal conversations with Diana Bacci, Vice President/Registrar at Eastern University, and Lisa Goodheart, attorney with Sugerman, Rogers, Barshak and Cohen in Boston, MA. These figures are rough estimates that can vary widely depending on the individual's background, proposed length of stay, and other factors.
6. Ibid.
7. Kevin McDonald, "Jewish Involvement in Shaping American Immigration Policy, 1881-1965: A Historical Review," California State Long Beach University, 2002. http://csulb.edu/~kmacd/books-immigration.html (accessed September 2007).
8. Ibid.
9. Sudarsan Raghavan, "War in Iraq Propelling a Massive Migration," *The Washington Post*, 2/4/07. http://www.washingtonpost.com/wp-dyn/content/article/2007/02/03/AR2007020301604.html (accessed September 2007).

10. Ibid.
11. Emma Lazarus, "The New Colossus," 1883.

Chapter 12: Crime

1. "Largest Increase in Prison and Jail Inmate Populations Since Midyear 2000," Department of Justice, Office of Justice Programs, 6/27/07. http://www.ojp.usdoj.gov/bjs/pub/press/pjim06pr.pdf (accessed October 2007).
2. Ibid.
3. "Largest Prison Inmate Increase Since 2000," CBS News, June 27, 2007. http://www.cbsnews.com/stories/2007/06/27/national/main2987952.shtml?source=RSSattr=U.S._2987952 (accessed October 2007).
4. Bureau of Justice Statistics, "Lifetime Likelihood of Going to State or Federal Prison," U.S. Department of Justice. http://www.ojp.usdoj.gov/bjs/abstract/llgsfp.htm (accessed October 2007).
5. Ibid.
6. "Bush Republicans Cut Law Enforcement Funding, Violent Crime Increases For Second Consecutive Year," Democratic Policy Committee, 9/26/07. http://democrats.senate.gov/dpc/dpc-new.cfm?doc_name=fs-110-1-150 (accessed October 2007).
7. According to a comparative analysis from the U.S. Census Bureau's records, in the year 2000, the total estimate of males 19-39 years of age was 41,127,000 and rose to roughly 41,577,000 in 2006. See "Age Sex and Groups: 2000," U.S. Census Bureau. http://factfinder.census.gov/servlet/QTTable?_bm=y&-geo_id=01000US&-qr_name=DEC_2000_SF1_U_QTP1&-ds_name=DEC_2000_SF1_U (accessed October 2007). See also "Age and Sex," U.S. Census Bureau. http://factfinder.census.gov/servlet/STTable?_bm=y&-geo_id=01000US&-qr_name=ACS_2006_EST_G00_S0101&-ds_name=ACS_2006_EST_G00_&-redoLog=false (accessed October 2007).
8. K. Michael Cummings, Anthony Brown and Richard O' Connor, "The Cigarette Controversy," Department of Health Behavior of Roswell Park Cancer Institute, 6/1/07. http://cebp.aacrjournals.org/cgi/content/abstract/16/6/1070 (accessed September 2007). See also "Connecticut's Lawsuit Against the Tobacco Companies Questions and Answers," CT Attorney General's Office press release, 7/18/96. http://www.ct.gov/AG/cwp/view.asp?A= 1771&Q=291160 (accessed September 2007).
9. Pratap Chatterjee, "The Thief of Baghdad," Alternet, 8/23/04. http://alternet.org/waroniraq/19620/ (accessed September 2007).
10. "Cheney's Halliburton Ties Remain," CBS News, 9/26/07. http://www.cbsnews.com/stories/2003/09/26/politics/main575356.shtml?source=search_story (accessed September 2007).
11. "Jack Abramoff" at Wikipedia.org. http://en.wikipedia.org/wiki/Jack_Abramoff (accessed September 2007).
12. "L.A. Hospital Employees Receive Training on 'Their Responsibilities' In Death of Patient," Freedom's Zone, 5/16/07. http://freedomszone.com/archives/2007/06/la_hospital_employees_receive.php (accessed September 2007).
13. Patricia Barry, "Why Drugs Cost Less Up North," AARP, June 2003. http://www.aarp.org/bulletin/prescription/a2003-08-12-whydrugs.html (accessed September 2007). See also "Prescription Drugs: Negotiation, Reimportation, Buying Pools and Other Important Reforms," The State PIRG Consumer Protection. http://www.pirg.org/consumer/import.htm (accessed September 2007); Don Oldenburg, "Prescription Prices: What's the Big Secret?" *The Washington Post*, 10/26/04. http://www.washingtonpost.com/wp-dyn/articles/A62807-2004Oct25.html (accessed September 2007).
14. "Los Angeles Accuses Hospital Giant of Dumping Homeless Patients in Skid Row," *USA Today*, 11/16/2006. http://www.usatoday.com/news/health/2006-11-16-kaiser_x.htm (accessed September 2007).

15. Charles Colson and Daniel Van Ness, *Convicted* (Westchester, IL: Crossway Books, 1992), p. 48.
16. From a personal conversation with Rob Acton, Executive Director, Cabrini Green Legal Clinic, July 2007.
17. George Jones and Matthew Moore, "Blair Opposes Execution of Saddam," *The Daily Telegraph*, 11/07/2006. http://www.telegraph.co.uk/news/main.jhtml?xml=/news/2006/11/06/usaddam 106.xml (accessed September 2007).
18. H.R. 261, "The Federal Prison Bureau Nonviolent Offender Relief Act of 2007." http:// thomas.loc.gov/cgi-bin/query/z?c110:H.R.261 (accessed October 2007).
19. Bureau of Justice Statistics, "State Prison Expenditures 2001," U.S. Department of Justice. http://ojp.usdoj.gov/bjs/pub/ascii/spe01.txt (accessed October 2007).
20. Dianne F. Herman, "The Rape Culture," in Jack Levin and Arnold Arluke (editors), *Sociology: Snapshots and Portraits of Society* (Thousand Oaks, CA: Pine Forge Press, 1996), pp. 50-53.
21. Tomas Borge, *Christianity and Revolution: Tomas Borge's Theology of Life*, translated by Andrew Roding (New York: Orbis Books, 1987), ch. 7.

Chapter 13: The Federal Budget

1. Robert Greenstein, "Despite the Rhetoric, Budget Would Make Nation's Fiscal Problems Worse, and Further Widen Inequality," Center on Budget and Policy Priorities, 3/28/07. http://www.cbpp.org/2-5-07bud.htm (accessed September 2007).
2. Aura Kanegis, "The Proposed Fiscal Year 2008 Budget: Little to Reflect Our Values," American Friends Service Committee, 2/7/07. http://afsc.org/locations/dc/documents/pro posedbudget.pdf (accessed September 2007).
3. Aviva Aron-Dine, "The Skewed Benefits of Tax Cuts, 2008-2017 with the Tax Cuts Extended, Top 1 Percent of Households Will Receive More Than $1 Trillion in Tax Benefits over the Next Decade," Center on Budget Policy and Priorities, 2/6/07. http://www.cbpp.org/2-5-07tax.htm (accessed September 2007).
4. Arloc Sherman, Sharon Parrott and Danilo Trisi, "President's Budget Would Cut Deeply into Important Public Services and Adversely Affect States," Center on Budget and Policy Priorities, 2/21/07. http://www.cbpp.org/2-21-07bud.pdf (accessed September 2007). See also Robert Greenstein, "Despite the Rhetoric, Budget Would Make Nation's Fiscal Problems Worse and Further Widen Equality," Center on Budget and Policy Priorities, 3/28/07. http://www.cbpp.org/2-5-07bud.htm (accessed September 2007); Sharon Parrott and Matt Fiedler, "President's Budget Calls for Deep Cuts in Wide Range of Domestic Programs: Cuts Start in 2008 and Grow Deeper Over Time," Center on Budget Policy and Priorities, 3/28/07. http://www.cbpp.org/2-8-07bud.htm (accessed September 2007).
5. Melanie Burney, "Camden School Shake-Up Likely," *Philadelphia Inquirer*, 7/9/07. http:// www.philly.com/inquirer/education/camden_schools/8385177.html (accessed September 2007).
6. Winnie Hu and Ford Fessenden, "Data Show Wide Differences in New Jersey School Spending," *The New York Times*, 3/24/07. http://www.nytimes.com/2007/03/24/nyregion/24spend.html (accessed September 2007).
7. William J. Bennett, *The Index of Leading Cultural Indicators* (New York: Broadway Books, 1999), p. 175. The American household watches television 7.12 hours per day. I have had conversations with Bruce Main, Executive Director of Urban Promise in Camden, NJ, who provided his estimate of at least 6 hours of viewing by a Camden child.
8. "Tax as You Go," *The Wall Street Journal*, January 5, 2007, p. A12. Text available at http:// www.house.gov/ hensarling/rsc/doc/CA_010807_tiahrttax.doc.
9. Richard Kogan, Matt Fiedler, Aviva Aron-Dine and James Horney, "The Long-Term Fiscal Outlook Is Bleak: Restoring Fiscal Sustainability Will Require Major Changes to Programs, Revenues, and the Nation's Health Care System," Center on Budget and Policy Priorities, 1/29/07. http://www.cbpp.org/1-29-07bud.htm (accessed September 2007).

10. Leighton Ku, Andy Schneider and Judy Solomon, "The Administration Again Proposes to Shift Federal Medicaid Costs to States," Center on Budget and Policy Priorities, 2/14/07. http://www.cbpp.org/2-14-07health.htm (accessed September 2007).
11. Sherman, Parrott and Trisi, "President's Budget Would Cut Deeply into Important Public Services and Adversely Affect States."
12. Jonathan Weisman, "Report Emphasizes Shortfall in Medicare," *The Washington Post*, 3/24/05. http://www.washingtonpost.com/wp-dyn/articles/A59227-2005Mar23.html (accessed September 2007). See also Chad Stone and Robert Greenstein, "What the 2007 Trustee's Report Shows About Social Security," Center on Budget Policy and Priorities, 4/24/07. http://www.cbpp.org/4-24-07socsec.htm (accessed September 2007).
13. Ibid.
14. Ibid.
15. Ibid. See also William Gale and Peter Orszag, "The Cost of Tax Cuts," *Minneapolis Star-Tribune*, 9/19/04. http://www.brookings.edu/views/articles/20040919galeorszag.htm (accessed September 2007).
16. "Report of the National Commission on Social Security Reform," Social Security Greenspan Commission, 01/83. http://www.ssa.gov/history/reports/gspan.html (accessed September 2007).
17. Martin Wolk, "Bush Pushes His Social Security Overhaul," MSNBC, February 16, 2005. http://www.msnbc.msn.com/id/6903273/ (accessed September 2007).
18. James Horney, "The Senate Budget Committee's Budget Plan—A Brief Analysis," Center on Budget Policy and Priorities, 3/19/07. http://www.cbpp.org/3-16-07bud.htm (accessed September 2007).
19. Ibid.
20. Ibid.
21. Ibid.
22. Ibid.
23. "List of Countries and Federations by Military Expenditures," Wikipedia.org. http://en.wikipedia.org/wiki/List_of_countries_by_military_expenditures (accessed September 2007).
24. "Budget Fact Sheet: Defense," The White House, 2007. www.whitehouse.gov/omb/pdf/defense-2008.pdf (accessed September 2007). See also American Friends Service Committee, "The Proposed Fiscal Year 2008 Budget," by Aura Kanegis, AFSC Washington Office Director, February 7, 2007, p. 2; Anne Scott Tyson, "Bush's Defense Budget Biggest Since Reagan Era," *The Washington Post*, February 6, 2007, p. A6. http://www.washingtonpost.com/wp-dyn/content/article/2007/02/05/AR2007020 501552.html (accessed September 2007).

Chapter 14: The Minimum Wage

1. Personal discussion in a counseling relationship with President Bill Clinton.
2. "The Uninsured: Americans at Risk," ConsumerReports.org, January 2004. Data from U.S. Census Bureau, 2002. http://www.consumerreports.org/cro/aboutus/mission/viewpoint/theuninsuredamericansatrisk104/ (accessed September 2007).
3. "Field Listing Unemployment Rate," U.S. Central Intelligence Agency. https://www.cia.gov/library/publications/the-world-factbook/fields/2129.html (accessed September 2007).

Chapter 15: Debtor Nation

1. Jonathan Shaw, "Debtor Nation," *Harvard Magazine*, July-August 2007, p. 48. http://www.harvardmagazine.com/2007/07/debtor-nation.html (accessed October 2007).
2. Ibid., p. 40.
3. Ibid.
4. Ibid., p. 44.
5. Ibid., p. 42.

6. Ibid.
7. Ibid.
8. Ibid., p. 40.
9. Ibid.
10. Ibid., p. 42.

Chapter 16: Wasteful Government

1. Jeannine Aversa, "Unemployment Rate Dips to 4.5 Percent," *The Washington Post*, March 9, 2007. http://www.washingtonpost.com/wp-dyn/content/article/2007/03/09/AR2007030900699.html.
2. Lou Dobbs, "Tax Cuts, Jobs and the Election," CNNMoney.com, November 3, 2003. http://money.cnn.com/2003/11/03/commentary/dobbs/dobbs/index.htm (accessed October 2007).
3. Steven R. Weisman, "Fed Chief Warns that Entitlement Growth Could Harm Economy," *The New York Times*, January 19, 2007. http://www.nytimes.com/2007/01/19/business/19fed.html?_r=1&oref=slogin (October 2007).
4. Bob Powers, "Nearly Half of All Americans Listen to Christian Radio," NRB. http://www.nrb.org/partner/Article_Display_Page/0,,PTID308778|CHID568026|CIID1985332,00.html (accessed September 2007).
5. Carol McGraw, "Focus on the Family Will Lay Off 30, Move 15 More to New Jobs," *The Colorado Springs Gazette,* September 11, 2007. http://www.msnbc.msn.com/id/20725308/ (accessed September 2007).
6. The late D. James Kennedy regularly made the fight against secularism a part of his telecasts.
7. Ronald D. Utt, "The Bridge to Nowhere: A National Embarrassment," The Heritage Foundation, WebMemo #889, October 20, 2005. http://www.heritage.org/Research/Budget/wm889.cfm (accessed September 2007). See also, Rebecca Clarren, "A Bridge to Nowhere," Salon.com, August 9, 2005. http://dir.salon.com/story/news/feature/2005/08/09/bridges/ (accessed September 2007).
8. This accusation is commonly reported to Mara Vanderslice, a political advisor for the Democratic Party.
9. Having established ministries in Camden, New Jersey, I have personally witnessed this discrimination. Our tutoring program, which serves more children than any other in the city has been repeatedly turned down for federal grant monies without justification.
10. David Kuo, "Please, Keep Faith," Beliefnet.com, 2006. http://www.beliefnet.com/story/160/story_16092_1.html (accessed September 2007).
11. David Kuo, *Tempting Faith: An Inside Story of Political Seduction* (New York: Free Press, 2006).
12. All of these facts were obtained from Richard Vignerie, Chairman of American Target Advertising, former publisher of *Conservative Digest* and former consultant for Steve Forbes's campaign for Republican nomination for the presidency. See also Daniel J. Mitchell, "A Brief Guide to the Flat Tax," The Heritage Foundation, Backgrounder #1866, July 7, 2005. http://www.her itage.org/Research/Taxes/bg1866.cfm (accessed September 2007).
13. Ibid.
14. Ibid.
15. Arianna Huffington made this statement at a gathering she convened during the Republican Convention held in Philadelphia in 2000.

Chapter 17: Political Lobbyists

1. "Colin C. Peterson: Campaign Finance/Money Contributions," Opensecrets.org, 12/31/06. http://www.opensecrets.org/politicians/summary.asp?cid=N00004558 (accessed September 2007). See also "Lawmakers Raise $2.2M in First Quarter," *USA Today*, 4/16/07. http://www.usatoday.com/news/washington/2007-04-16-demsmoney-table_n.htm (accessed September 2007).

2. "Peterson Announces Farm Bill Agreement," Congressman Collin Peterson Minnesota's 7th Congressional District, 4/22/02. http://collinpeterson.house.gov/press/107th/farmbill_agreement.htm (accessed September 2007).
3. Ellyn Ferguson, "House Panel Juggles Competing Interests to Write Farm Policy Bill," *USA Today*, 7/17/07. http://www.usatoday.com/news/washington/2007-07-15-farmbill_n.htm (accessed September 2007). See also Ken Dilanian, "Billions Go to House Panel Members' Districts," *USA Today*, 7/25/07. http://www.usatoday.com/news/washington/2007-07-25-farmbill_n.htm (accessed September 2007).
4. Ibid.
5. George B. Tindall and David E. Shi, *America: A Narrative History*, Vol. II (New York: W. W. Norton & Co., 4th ed., 1996), pp. 1548-1552.
6. Rep. Henry A. Waxman, "Pharmaceutical Industry Profits Increase by Over $8 Billion After Medicare Prescription Drug Plan Goes into Effect," Ranking Minority Leader, Committee on Government Reform, U.S. House of Representatives, September 2006. http://oversight.house.gov/documents/20060919115623-70677.pdf (accessed September 2007). See also Marcia Angell, "The Truth About the Drug Companies," *New York Review of Books*, vol. 51, no. 12, July 15, 2004. http://www.nybooks.com/articles/17244 (accessed September 2007). For the growing problem of prescription drug affordability among the poor and elderly, see Maria C. Reeds, Issue Brief, "Update on Americans' Access to Prescription Drugs," Center for Studying Health System Change, No. 95, May 2005. http://www.hschange.org/CONTENT/738/738.pdf (accessed September 2007).
7. Neil Osterweil, "Buying Drugs Across the Border," WebMD. http://www.webmd.com/healthy-aging/features/buying-drugs-across-border (accessed September 2007).
8. "Health Insurance Coverage," National Coalition on Health Care. http://www.nchc.org/facts/coverge.shtml (accessed September 2007).
9. Ken Silverstein, "Send Lawyers, Guns and Money: Lobbying and the Merchants of Death," excerpt from the book *Washington on $10 Million a Day* (Monroe, ME: Common Courage Press, 1998). http://www.thirdworldtraveler.com/Political_Corruption/LobbyingMerchantsDeath.html (accessed September 2007).
10. "Budget Fact Sheet: Defense," The White House, 2007. www.whitehouse.gov/omb/pdf/defense-2008.pdf (accessed September 2007). See also American Friends Service Committee, "The Proposed Fiscal Year 2008 Budget," by Aura Kanegis, AFSC Washington Office Director, February 7, 2007, p. 2; Anne Scott Tyson, "Bush's Defense Budget Biggest Since Reagan Era," *The Washington Post*, February 6, 2007, p. A6. http://www.washingtonpost.com/wp-dyn/content/article/2007/02/05/AR2007020501552.html (accessed September 2007).
11. Jonathan Karp, "In Military-Spending Boom, Expensive Pet Projects Prevail," *The Wall Street Journal* online, June 16, 2006. http://online.wsj.com/article/SB115042343540682069.html (accessed September 2007). See also The Project on Government Oversight's Defense Archive, which details cases of wasteful defense spending. http://www.pogo.org/p/x/archivedefense.html#defensespending (accessed September 2007).
12. Tom Abate, "Military Waste Under Fire," *San Francisco Chronicle*, May 18, 2003. http://www.sfgate.com/cgi-bin/article.cgi?file=/c/a/2003/05/18/MN251738.DTL (accessed September 2007).
13. Admiral Hyman C. Rickover, "Corporate Power and Military Corruption," Joint Economic Committee, U.S. Congress, January 28, 1982, provides an overview of the ways the government is defrauded on a regular basis.
14. Elizabeth Becker, "A Nation at War: Reconstruction Contracts; 2 Democrats Call for Scrutiny of Bidding to Reconstruct Iraq," *The New York Times*, April 9, 2003. http://query.nytimes.com/gst/fullpage.html?res=9F00E4DA1E38F93AA35757C0A9659C8B63&n=Top%2fReference%2fTimes%20Topics%2fOrganizations%2fG%2fGovernment%20A

ccountability%20Office (accessed September 2007). See also Diana B. Henriques, "Competing for Work in Post War Iraq," *The New York Times*, April 10, 2007. http://query.nytimes.com/gst/fullpage.html?res=9F03EFDA1F38F933A25757C0A9659C8B63&n=Top%2fReference%2fTimes%20Topics%2fOrganizations%2fG%2fGovernment%20Accountability%20Office (accessed September 2007); Elizabeth Becker, "A Nation at War: Reconstruction; Details Given on Contract Halliburton Was Awarded," *The New York Times*, April 11, 2003. http://query.nytimes.com/gst/fullpage.html?res=9B04EED9173BF932A25757C0A9659C8B63&n=Top%2fReference%2fTimes%20Topics%2fOrganizations%2fG%2fGovernment%20Accountability%20Office (accessed September 2007).

15. Michele Steinberg, "Will Stolen Iraq Oil Funds and Deals for Cronies Force Cheney Impeachment?" *Executive Intelligence Review*, July 15, 2005. http://www.larouchepub.com/other/2005/3228halliburton.html (accessed September 2007).
16. Jane Merriman, "Investors Drive Brent Oil Above Plentiful U.S. Crude," Reuters, March, 21, 2007. http://www.reuters.com/article/reutersEdge/idUSL2121547120070321 (accessed September 2007).
17. "The Hungry Dragon: China's Material Needs (China's insatiable appetite for raw materials)," *The Economist*, February 2004. http://www.economist.com/business/displaystory.cfm?story_id=2446908 (accessed September 2007).
18. John W. Schoen, "U.S. Refiners Stretch to Meet Demand," MSNBC, November 22, 2004. http://www.msnbc.msn.com/id/6019739/ (accessed October 2007). See also the transcript of President Bush's remarks, "President Discusses Refining Capacity in Biloxi, Mississippi," Office of the Press Secretary, April 27, 2007. http://www.whitehouse.gov/news/releases/2006/04/20060427-12.html (accessed September 2007).

Chapter 18: Campaign Finance

1. Mark J. Green, James M. Fallows and David R. Zwick, *Who Runs Congress?* (New York: Bantam Books, 1972), ch. 8. See also Paula Dwyer and Douglas Harbrecht, "Congress: It Doesn't Work, Let's Fix It," in George McKenna and Stanley Feingold (editors), *Taking Sides* (New York: Dushkin Publishing, 8th ed., 1993), p. 85.

Chapter 19: The Right Kind of Candidate

1. Mohammad Ayatollahi Tabaar, "Iran: The Road Not Taken," *Asia Times*, 8/20/03. http://www.atimes.com/atimes/Middle_East/EH20Ak02.html (accessed September 2007).
2. Peter J. Goldberg, "The Politics of the Allende Overthrow in Chile," *Political Science Quarterly*, Vol. 90, No. 1, Spring 1975, pp. 93ff. See also "CIA Acknowledges Involvement in Allende's Overthrow, Pinochet's Rise," CNN.com, September 19, 2000. http://archives.cnn.com/2000/WORLD/americas/09/19/us.cia.chile.ap/ (accessed September 2007).

Chapter 20: On Earth as It Is in Heaven

1. "Digesting Digest's WCC Attack: Reader's Digest; World Council of Churches," *Christian Century*, 2/3/93. http://findarticles.com/p/articles/mi_m1058/is_n4_v110/ai_13509817 (accessed September 2007).
2. Noam Chomsky, *What Uncle Sam Really Wants*, (Odonian Press, 1992).
3. "Vietnam Online: Timeline," PBS, 3/29/05. http://www.pbs.org/wgbh/amex/vietnam/timeline/index.html (accessed September 2007).
4. "Oxfam America: U.S. Bullies Poor Countries on Trade; Double-Standard Pushed on Developing Countries to Open Markets; U.S. Maintains Subsidies, Protections in Trade Agreements from DR-CAFTA to WTO," CommonDreams.org News Center, 4/11/05. http://www.commondreams.org/news2005/0411-03.htm (accessed September 2007).
5. I was in Pretoria in July 2003 when President Bush made a visit and spoke before the South African Parliament. I personally witnessed farmers from South Africa stage a rally of several thousand to protest the way free trade, coupled with U.S. government subsidies for American farmers, was driving them out of business.

6. To find out more about SPEAK, visit www.speak.org.uk or http://groups.eastern.edu/~speak/.
7. "USA Patriot Act," American Civil Liberties Union, 11/14/03. http://www.aclu.org/safe free/resources/17343res20031114.html (accessed September 2007).
8. Ibid.
9. Ibid.
10. "U.S. Spying Broader than Acknowledged: Report," CTV.ca, 12/24/05. http://www.ctv.ca/servlet/ArticleNews/story/CTVNews/20051224/spying_report_051224?s_name=&no_ads= (accessed September 2007).
11. A survey of issues raised by the Patriot Act is provided by Frank Gaffney, *War Footing* (Annapolis, MD: Naval Institute Press, 2006), pp. 78-82.